real
chocolate

real
chocolate

OVER 50 INSPIRING RECIPES FOR
CHOCOLATE INDULGENCE

Chantal Coady

quadrille

I would like to dedicate this book to my children, Fergus and Millie, and their cousins, Cesar, Charlie, Emily, Frances, Jamie, Jo Jo, Laura, Maddie, Miranda, Nick, Peter and Toby, and my godchildren, Jessica, Camila and Theodora.

Editor & project manager: Lewis Esson
Design, art direction & styling: Françoise Dietrich
Production: Tracy Hart

Illustrations: Chantal Coady
Photography: Richard Foster
(except for the photograph of the author on page 19, which is by Cindy Palmano for *The Face* magazine)
Home economist: Jane Suthering assisted by Thom Hughes

First published in 2003 by
Quadrille Publishing Limited,
Alhambra House,
27-31 Charing Cross Road,
London WC2H OLS

This paperback edition first published in 2004

Cataloguing in Publication Data: a catalogue record for this book is available from the British Library

ISBN 1 84400 081 8

Printed and bound in Singapore

contents

introduction

Almost twenty years have gone by since I first opened Rococo, and things have come a long way. I still love chocolate with a passion, and I am so happy to have been able to carve my own niche in this extraordinary business, which continues to give so much pleasure to so many people. I really enjoy the opportunity to experiment with flavours and types of chocolate in a constantly evolving creative process. My hope is that this book will allow you to share some of that enjoyment.

Chantal Coady

London September 2002

chocolate facts

As I became more serious about chocolate issues, and I started to ask questions about the established order of the chocolate business, I opened a can of worms. I felt that I had to offer a choice about the kind of chocolate people consumed and to give them the information they needed to make their choices. It is not that I want to dictate the kind of chocolate eaten, but I believe everyone should at least be able to taste the real thing and decide for themselves. In 1986, I started the Campaign for Real Chocolate, to counter the multinational chocolate makers argument that the addition of vegetable and other fats in chocolate was quite acceptable. At that time the EU was trying to have this type of chocolate confectionery renamed 'vegelate', which I found an apt description of the low-grade product masquerading as something else. The long-running battle was finally resolved with a fudge: this kind of bar may be sold into the European market as 'Family Milk Chocolate', the ingredients primarily sugar and fat, with a lot of milk and not very much cocoa or cocoa butter. What my campaign has been trying to establish is the minimum acceptable level of cocoa, that cocoa butter is the only legitimate fat in a chocolate bar, and that sugar shouldn't be the primary ingredient.

In 1990, the Campaign's aims were refocused with the launch of The Chocolate Society, which I started with Nicola Porter. The message about Real Chocolate was widely trumpeted by the national press, and at last it seemed to gain support. A ground-swell revolt against the bog-standard sugar- and fat-laden British chocolate had started, and consumers began to read the ingredients labels before purchasing a bar of chocolate. I suppose it is inevitable that sometimes only part of the message gets through, and it seems this is why the percentage of the cocoa content became the deciding factor. Of course, it is one determining factor, but only one, and the origin and quality of the beans are even more important. I have tasted many bars of chocolate with a high cocoa content that have been quite filthy, with burnt aromas and all sorts of other bad 'notes'. I hope that this section of my book will give you all the information you need to help you make your own informed judgements on chocolate.

the history of chocolate

There are certain moments in the history of mankind when quantum leaps are made, such as when nomadic stone-age men settled long enough in one place to plant crops and domesticate animals; the invention of the wheel is another such moment, as was the discovery that the addition of lime to cornmeal, when soaked in water overnight, softened the tough outer husk of the cereal to make a protein-rich dough. The word for this process is nixtamalization, which comes from the language of the Central American Olmecs, whose diet was transformed by the process. The Olmec people settled the fertile lowlands of the Mexican gulf, cultivating maize, chillies, avocados, pumpkins and beans, and it was almost certainly the Olmecs who first cultivated the cocoa tree (*Theobroma cacao*).

The Olmec civilization lasted from around 1500BC to 400BC, declining and eventually vanishing. The secret of nixtamalization was passed on to the Mayas, Toltecs and Aztecs. The Spanish did not seem to understand or adopt it. They brought back and cultivated maize in Europe but, in spite of heavy grinding in mills to soften the grains, diseases caused by protein deficiencies such as pellagra were widespread among populations for many years. By the time Cortés arrived with his bunch of conquistadors in 'New Spain' the by-then dominant Aztecs were a stratified society with huge populations living in an organized and democratic order, with an established infrastructure of merchants who distributed produce to the markets all around the country. The Mayas were banished to the Yucatan and living as slaves, growing the most important Aztec commodity – cacao. Cacao was made into a cold spicy gruel that was an integral part of all their rituals and ceremonies.

chocolate in Europe

Hernán Cortés can take the credit for successfully taking cocoa to Europe. He could see its importance as a cash crop, for in Mexico the cocoa bean had a monetary value, and was used in the place of small coins. Cortés had been searching for the gold of El Dorado, but he quickly realized that cocoa was a renewable source of 'money'. He took the beans and planted them in Haiti, Trinidad and, it is believed, on the island of São Tomé. From there they were taken to the Ivory Coast, where much of the world's 'bulk' cocoa is grown. It was Cortés, too, who adapted the Aztec recipe for preparing chocolate gruel, so that the cold, fatty and spicy drink, which some chroniclers called 'a wash fitter for hogs', became a hot drink, with the addition of sugar, vanilla and cinnamon, that appealed so much to the European palate.

From its introduction to the royal court in Spain in the sixteenth century, cocoa remained a closely guarded secret for about a hundred years. Then through a series of strategic royal marriages made to secure the future of the Holy Roman Empire (later to become the Austro-Hungarian Empire), the taking of chocolate spread through the palaces of Europe. At first chocolate was drunk only in the privacy of the bedchamber, at breakfast time. Some critics were alarmed at the power of this beverage, which was said to be intoxicating. It was, in fact, the first alkaloid to be introduced into Europe, before tea and coffee.

During the seventeenth and eighteenth centuries it remained the preserve of royalty and the aristocracy, as it was a highly taxed commodity. At this time cocoa was sold under special licence by royal apothecaries, who regarded it more as a medicine than a foodstuff. Cocoa has always been a precious commodity so, quite naturally, whenever there is money to be made, there will be a fraudster trying to make a fast buck, and cocoa is no exception to this rule. There are accounts of Aztec cocoa beans being hollowed out and filled with earth, then passed off as counterfeit money. In Europe, brick dust was commonly found in the cocoa being sold by the less scrupulous merchants, and today the practice of adulteration continues in more insidious ways.

Cocoa was also an important commodity in the slave triangle. Ships would set sail from Liverpool and Bristol, laden with ironmongery and textiles produced by the mills of the Industrial Revolution, and exchange them with West African chiefs for a cargo of slaves. This human cargo was transported to the West Indies, where the slaves were used to labour on sugar and cocoa plantations. A cargo of tropical hardwood, like mahogany, or sugar, rum and cocoa was loaded on to the ships for the last leg of the trip back. There is an early account of pirates who, having seized a ship, jettisoned its cargo of cocoa beans believing them to be sheep droppings.

It was not until the middle of the nineteenth century (1852 in England) that taxation was slashed from 10 per cent (two out of the 20 shillings in every pound sterling) to one penny per pound in weight of cocoa. It was also around this time that the revolution in the manufacture of cocoa came about. The Dutchman Van Houten patented the cocoa press and the process of alkalizing cocoa, both of which removed the excess fatty components of cocoa, making it much more readily soluble as a drink. Then came the Swiss Rudolf Lindt, who invented the conch (see page 17) and 'eating chocolate' as we know it today. At this stage, the current big boys came on the scene: the Cadburys, the Frys and the Rowntrees in England, Nestlé in Switzerland, Hershey and Bakers in the USA, following in the footsteps of Van Houten and Lindt. Many early industrial producers of chocolate were Quakers and, being barred from the professions they might have

followed, they became industrialists. The Cadburys and Milton Hershey built model villages for their workforces, educated their children and provided health care and near-Utopian conditions for the time. Chocolate was also heralded as a pure and healthy alternative to the dreaded gin, which had ruined the lives of so many working people before them. Chocolate was even marketed as 'flesh forming' which, at the time, was as powerful a marketing tool as 'low-fat' is today.

chocolate in the twentieth century

Ironically, it was these noble Quaker ideals that laid the foundations of our now degraded industrial food production. The world most of us inhabit has too much food, largely of very dubious quality. Although there is no intrinsic reason why large-scale production should necessarily mean poor-quality products, it invariably does. Profit margins are the driving forces of these industries, and any small tweak in the manufacturing process can result in a huge increase on the bottom line.

Probably the blackest day in chocolate history came in World War II when Milton Hershey invented a special non-melting chocolate to send to American troops in the Far East in their ration packs. The innovation involved removing the cocoa butter, and replacing it with a waxy compound with a much higher melting point. The result was seized upon by chocolate manufacturers in Europe, particularly in the UK, Ireland and Denmark, and has stuck in the throats of chocolate lovers ever since. For many people, this is the norm, apart from being the only chocolate they've ever experienced, but a far cry from the real thing! On a happier note, in many parts of Europe the tradition of artisan food production has remained unaffected by the Industrial Revolution, particularly for chocolate-making. Although many of these traditions are under threat, there are also as many supporters. There are hundreds of small chocolate makers in France, and they can also be found readily in Spain, Italy, Austria, Germany, Belgium and Holland.

But to return to the history of chocolate, I now realize it is littered with inaccuracies that have been passed from one generation to the next in an unintentional game of Chinese whispers. Each writer, trusting unquestioningly material they have gleaned from respected treatises. I am not the first writer to have fallen into this trap. Indeed, in my first book I, too, declared that the Aztecs used cinnamon to flavour their chocolate. The Spanish may have introduced them to this spice, but there is no evidence of trade between the Spice Islands of the East Indies and the Aztecs or Mayans. I am going to gloss over much of the early history of chocolate because there is finally a book, the definitive chocolate bible, *The True History of Chocolate* by Sophie and Michael Coe (Thames & Hudson, London 1996) which says it all, and unlike the other histories, this one has gone back to the original sources, so no danger of received fiction in this book - read it!

chocolate from bean to bar

Children brought up in Western consumer societies are so far removed from the reality of food production they may be forgiven for believing that milk starts its life in a carton and has nothing to do with cows. In its own way, chocolate is another foodstuff the origins of which are shrouded in mystery. We'll never know who first decided to eat this fruit, or who transformed it into 'cacao' or cocoa, but I will try to demystify the process that transforms it into slabs of eating chocolate.

beginning with the bean

Cocoa trees grow in a very narrow belt 10–20 degrees either side of the equator. They are fragile and need constant rainfall, warmth and shelter from the wind and sun. Basically there are two genetic types of cocoa – Forastero and Criollo. Forastero is the bulk cocoa grown for the commodity markets. With round pods, it is a high-yielding, hardy variety, the flavour of which is not considered to be particularly fine. Criollo is the original fine cocoa bean, a fragile – and now an endangered – species. The pods are normally red and elongated, and the flavour very fruity, redolent of ripe raspberries, redcurrants, and citrus fruit. At present this species of bean accounts for less than 5 per cent of the world's cocoa production.

Said to have been the result of natural cross-pollination after a hurricane in Trinidad in the eighteenth century, Trinitario is the name given to a hybrid cross of the Criollo and Forastero. This variety is highly regarded by cocoa experts, as it has an excellent flavour with predominant green notes; apple, melon, oak, and balsam. There are many other hybrid beans, the best of which are fine in flavour and more robust than the Criollo bean.

It may be helpful to think of cocoa beans in the same terms as coffee. At the extreme ends of the coffee scale, Arabica and Robusta beans. Arabica (equivalent to Criollo) are regarded as the best, and it would be criminal to roast them black and hide their delicate flavour. Robusta coffee beans (equivalent to Forastero), however, are almost always highly roasted and used to make very strong espresso coffee. Most of the hybrid cocoa beans fall into the category of 'fine and flavour' beans, for which a premium is paid and due care is taken with their roasting, etc.

transforming the cocoa bean into a commodity

Cocoa is often grown alongside 'shade trees', referred to as 'mothers', such as coconut, banana or plantains. The ripe cocoa pods, which come in many shapes, sizes and colours (generally looking like rugby balls up to 30cm long), are harvested with great care. A machete is used to cut the pod from the tree trunk, and the knife must be cleaned after each cut, in order to prevent disease being spread in the humid growing conditions on the plantations. The pod is slashed open and the many small white fruit are piled on a mat of plantain leaves. The mound of beans is then covered with more leaves and left to ferment for seven days. Soft white flesh, which tastes a little like rambutan or mangosteen, surrounds the glossy dark seed, which is, in fact, the cocoa bean. The sweet flesh provides the sugar for the natural fermentation process that allows the beans to develop their characteristic chocolatey flavour. The residue of the fruit evaporates, and leaves behind traces of acetic acid.

The beans are then sun-dried. This part of the process can be problematic, as cocoa is grown in the rain forest, so daily downpours are the norm. Some growers have roll-on covers, a bit like the ones used to cover cricket pitches. Others resort to oven-drying, which is not usually the solution. Beans dried in this way are often tainted with smoke, which annihilates the fine flavour of the cocoa beans. The dried beans are graded and sorted, and put into sacks to be transported to the end-user. Good cocoa buyers will take a sample of around 100 beans from each sack, and count how many bad beans are found. Beans are rejected if they are mouldy or have started to sprout. The beans are then shipped to chocolate factories all around the world, where they will be transformed into the dark and delicious chocolate bars that we love so much.

the chocolate-making process

At the factory, the beans are checked for quality before being roasted. Roasting is a great skill, as the beans need to be roasted at a temperature of 120–140°C, to result in beans with a wonderful intense flavour. The art is ensuring that the beans are roasted long enough to bring out the flavour, while being careful not to burn the beans. The next process is known as winnowing, similar to separating wheat from chaff. The outer layer of the cocoa bean is blown away (and collected to become mulch for gardens), while the inner seed will be transformed into chocolate.

The next stage depends on what sort of chocolate it is destined to become. 'Fast' chocolate will be made quickly (in around 12 hours) – often the cocoa butter will be removed and replaced with other fats, as well as other artificial additives. 'Slow' chocolate will now be milled through a series of heavy metal rollers, and then further refined in conches, which pummel it between granite rollers at a temperature of 50–80°C for up to a week. The conch, named after the shell, was invented by Rodolfe Lindt in 1880. The longer chocolate is conched or refined, the smaller the particle size in the mouth. The finest chocolate will have particles measuring around 18-20 microns, so small as to be indiscernible to the palate. Also, the more slowly the chocolate is refined, the more acetic acid will evaporate and the mellower the chocolate will become.

and what is added in the process?

The finest chocolate will have extra cocoa butter added to make the chocolate even smoother and quicker to melt in the mouth. Normally, sugar is added to the chocolate, the quantity depends on the type of chocolate. Good dark chocolate will have around 30 per cent sugar, while fast chocolate may have up to 80 per cent. Milk chocolate will have milk added, in the form of milk 'crumb' or condensed milk. The milk crumb gives a slightly cheesy or farmyard flavour to the chocolate. British and American chocolate are made with crumb, whereas Swiss and other European chocolate is made from the condensed milk (invented by Henri Nestlé), which gives a much smoother, creamier texture. White chocolate is made from cocoa butter, milk and sugar, but doesn't contain any dry cocoa matter.

Cocoa butter substitutes are used widely in 'fast' chocolates. These are made from hydrogenated vegetable fats, such as palm, rape or soya oil, karite or mahua (illipe) butter, all of which are less expensive than cocoa butter. The effect of hydrogenation is to turn oils into solid fats by changing their molecular structure. In the process, normally quite healthy fatty acids are changed into trans fatty acids which can inhibit the body's ability to absorb good fatty acids. They are sometimes called fractionated oils on labels, to disguise them.

These fats also have a higher melting point than cocoa butter, which helps to stabilize the chocolate in warm conditions. In my opinion, there can never be any justification for the addition of these fats to replace cocoa butter. Non-cocoa butter fats do not melt at blood temperature, and these solid particles leave a greasy residue that sticks to the palate, the effect is cloying.

Cocoa butter is a unique fat. It is saturated, and yet behaves like an unsaturated fat. It contains oleic acid and, like olive oil, has been shown to reduce blood cholesterol levels. It also melts at just below blood temperature, as you'll know if you've ever held chocolate in your hand. The melting point is one of the most remarkable things about cocoa butter, as it melts on the tongue, it feels cool, it transforms the chocolate into a liquid which penetrates the taste buds and releases the volatile aromas up into the nose.

the genesis of Rococo

'Whatever made you think of opening a chocolate shop?' I have lost count of the number of people who've asked me that. To me the answer is so obvious I am amazed that anyone need ask. I have always been obsessed by chocolate, as far back as I can remember, and I thought that everyone dreamed of opening their own chocolate shop. Perhaps they did, when they were small, but then forgot about it or got sensible and decided to follow conventional careers. My dream was recurrent; many a time I walked through landscapes from *Charlie and the Chocolate Factory*, where the trees were swathed in sweets, blades of grass made from soft minty sugar, and rivers filled with molten chocolate. Each time I picked the sweets, gathered them in my skirts and returned home to hide them under my pillow, so that they would be there when I awoke. So vivid were these dreams, so bitter the disappointment on awaking and finding nothing.

I suppose in a way I deviated from my childhood fantasy when I went to art school, but it was there that I was given my dream ticket to chocolate heaven, or so I thought. I was offered a holiday job in the confectionery department of Harrods, at that time the archetypal British department store, staffed mainly by veterans who had worked there for at least 40 years. My immediate superior was a vodka-soaked tyrant who refused to give carrier bags to the day-trippers buying Mars bars. In spite of having a wonderful array of the finest chocolates available at that time, the atmosphere in the department was funereal, and the customers were largely treated with contempt. No one seemed to realize that they were purveying probably the finest handmade chocolates available in London. To me they were a revelation to behold and taste, and everyone I gave them to (I had a generous staff discount) was in raptures. Surely I was not alone in understanding that this chocolate had the power to transport the most hardened individual.

Everyone thought I was crazy when I said I was going to open my own chocolate shop. I saw a niche for something completely different – along the lines of a French *boutique de chocolat* – which would allow the customer to indulge in their wildest chocolate dreams, and no one managed to talk me out of it. I did a 10-week 'Start Your Own Business' Course, sponsored by the Manpower Services Commission, and was 23 when my bank manager agreed to lend me cash to start up. As I was penniless, my dear mother secured the loan with her house. Was this an act of supreme indulgence on her part, or did she believe I had inherited the female entrepreneurial streak from her side of the family (her mother and grandmother had both had shops)? For my part, business failure just wasn't a possibility, due to a mixture of blind faith and youthful chutzpah.

the dream becomes reality

I found a shop in the King's Road, which I felt was the perfect location. The type of punter on the street was very mixed: punks extorting money from Japanese tourists who took their photographs, the privileged Chelsea children (who bought, sold and consumed serious drugs in the local hostelries) and the residents who were to become the hard core of my clientele. Having vowed never to sell rose or violet creams, I had to buck up my ideas fast if I was going to keep the Establishment happy. I managed to persuade small, family chocolate makers to supply me with a range of handmade chocolate and Easter eggs, and also found suppliers of sugared almonds and other delicacies at the huge trade fair in Cologne. I certainly had no idea about how actually to make chocolates at that time, but I did now have an idea about what was good, even if my attitude to customer service was somewhat remiss.

Opening for trade three weeks before Easter nearly killed me. However, with the help of many kind people, including suppliers, who probably thought I was mad or a rich kid on a whim, somehow I managed to pull it all together. To begin with I ran the shop with the help of my brother and sister, but we spent as much time bickering as serving customers, so after a while they went their separate ways. I had one salutary experience in the first month of opening when I was quoted in the business section of *The Sunday Times* in response to the question 'What is the worst thing about running you own business?' replying, 'You could say we get a fair number of insufferable old bags in here.' I was definitely in

post-Harrods trauma, and fortunately only one young man took me to task over it saying, 'You might have been talking about MY mother!'

Luckily, few of the people who did read the piece ever identified themselves as being 'old bags', and most seemed amused by the *faux pas*. Soon I was a reformed character, and when someone was particularly rude or obnoxious, I would smile extra sweetly, never rise to the bait, and gradually there was a sea change. My favourite old lady, Miss Biddy Cook, one of the fiercest 'old bags', even apologized for her early behaviour, when she had taken every opportunity to get under my skin, and failed miserably, it made my day when she said, 'My Dear, I am so ashamed about how I used to behave when you first opened. I really did not believe that you stood a chance...'

With the help of my art school friends, Frank Taylor and Kitty Arden, I transformed the interior of the shop into a theatrical stage set inspired by the word 'rococo'. The walls were stippled in candy-floss pink, and so was my hair. I found the only person in England who could make a chandelier out of sugar, and I gradually transformed myself into an eighteenth-century stage character, with punk overtones. This all sounds rather ridiculous now, but at the time it seemed the right thing to do and everyone seemed to love it. What was right, though, was my feeling that most people could share my passion for real chocolate, and that by following this conviction I was capable of changing the perception of chocolate for countless individuals.

The word 'rococo' started to have deeper resonance for me and the business as I discovered that there was a Rococo period in London, and much of it based around the area in which I lived and worked. There were the Chelsea Potters, who made exquisite platters covered in shells and crustacea, the Ranelagh and Vauxhall Pleasure Gardens, where Handel performed his operas, and the Huguenot silk weavers who took refuge in Spitalfields away from the political persecution in France. I played only baroque music or opera in the shop, and became something of a 'barocky', and so was able to add a musical dimension to the Rococo experience.

the inspiration of Eurochocolate

In 1994, I was asked to write a guide to the world's best chocolate makers. This was a pretty tall order, as the publisher did not even have a database of chocolate makers, and I had only weeks to do the research, taste the chocolates and write up the book. It was a wonderful challenge, and with the help of the Comitato del Cioccolato who were launching 'Eurochocolate' for the first time, I met many small and medium-sized chocolate makers who had been brought together in

Perugia, Italy. The difference between this event and the many other chocolate-themed occasions that I have attended over the years was that it was driven by real passion not commercial gain.

Started by a maverick architect-cum-hotelier, Eugenio Guarducci, everyone was thrown together in a chaotic maelstrom. I made many firm friends that year, and have returned every year since, although sadly the event has now been hijacked by the city council of Perugia, who see it as a gravy train to bring in thousands of visitors from all over Italy. The Corso Vannucci, a huge medieval boulevard, was so full last year, I could picture a public execution, only here the crowds gathered around the scaffolds were baying for chocolate not blood. The other thing that surprised and delighted me was the generosity of spirit in which all the chocolate makers shared their recipes and secret tips. In some ways it is like giving a musician a score – each one will produce a different rendering of the piece, depending on the musical instrument or raw material, the degree of virtuosity and the emotion that goes into the performance. The recipes themselves are merely the starting point.

Rococo today

I was so inspired by what I witnessed in Italy in 1994 that I decided it was time for Rococo to get serious and start producing as much as possible in-house. I had a little knowledge about the technical side of chocolate making, but could see that many of the best chocolate makers were, in fact, trained in a completely different discipline, and were self-taught.

I gave a very basic training to Joanna Gaskell, our new chocolate maker, who pretty quickly knew much more than I did about tempering chocolate and making truffles. We built a tiny chocolate kitchen in my house, and soon we needed another chocolate maker. Today Ruth Morgan, who originally trained as a sculptor and designer, has now joined Jo.

The kitchen is really too small now and we are considering a new space. There we will be able to produce a larger range of chocolate, but still all made by hand. Rococo has jumped through the necessary hoops to get Organic Certification on the Artisan Bars, made using really fine organic chocolate and different herbs and spices, combined to achieve balance and flavour.

the truth about real chocolate

Real chocolate and 'fast' chocolate are very distant relations. I use the word 'fast' to differentiate the kind of industrial low-grade chocolate readily available and normally consumed as fast food.

real chocolate is actively good for you

Among the purposes of this book is to give real chocolate a positive image and to allow everyone to feel good about eating and enjoying it. It is one of the most nutritious and easily digested foods known. It contains a multitude of vitamins (A_1, B_1, B_2, C, D and E), minerals (calcium, potassium, sodium, magnesium, iron, zinc, copper, chromium and phosphorous) and complex alkaloids, all of which enhance health and well-being. The iron in chocolate also comes in a form 93 per cent useable by the body, the oxalic acid helping bond the iron and calcium so it is bio-available.

Real chocolate is low in sugar and has a low glycaemic index, meaning it keeps you feeling full for longer and helps keep your blood glucose levels steady. The glycaemic index of chocolate is 49 (45 for milk chocolate) and anything under 50 is considered low; crisps, biscuits, white bread and other refined carbohydrates have a high glycaemic index. There is strong evidence that replacing desserts with good chocolate can actually help weight loss and diabetes (see *A Chocolate a Day Keeps the Doctor Away* by Dr John Ashton and Suzy Ashton, Souvenir Press, London 2002).

There is a naturally occurring antidepressant in chocolate called phenylethylamine (PEA) which increases the serotonin levels in the brain. It can induce a euphoric state, as well as boosting energy levels and mental alertness. PEAs are found in 'love addicted' women. Low PEA levels are found in people who are depressed. Chocolate affects the hormones in the brain in a similar way to morphine, and so can relieve pain. Prozac is the man-made chemical used to treat depression by raising serotonin levels; it also has many well-documented side effects and is highly addictive. Real chocolate, however, acts as an instant antidepressant. Even its smell can have a calming effect on the brain. Chocolate also contains theobromine and valeric acid. The former is a stimulant similar to caffeine, with a chemical composition that has only one atom different but is weaker in its action. It stimulates the brain, muscles and central nervous system, and has also been shown to lower blood pressure.

Chocolate is also rich in flavinoids (also found in red wine) and other chemical compounds known to reduce the likelihood of deep vein thrombosis and strokes. Although red wine is excellent in moderate amounts, alcohol can be dangerous, but I have never heard of anyone being killed by eating real chocolate. Cocoa butter has been proven to lower blood cholesterol levels, and chocolate is rich in antioxidants, which help to destroy the unhealthy free radicals and boost the immune system, two of the most important factors in preventing cancer.

Chocolate is even used as a homeopathic remedy, indicated for feelings of hostility, especially when mothers feel anger and frustration towards their offspring. The effect is to restore the nurturing mother side, and to promote a general sense of well-being. (Interestingly, one theory why we love chocolate so much from an early age is that in many respects white chocolate is the closest thing to human breast milk.) The other surprising finding is that cocoa possesses antibacterial properties, which help to prevent tooth decay. It seems that most dentists are agreed that even chocolate containing sugar is significantly less harmful than sweets (like lollipops or boiled sweets) in relation to dental caries.

'fast' chocolate

'Fast' chocolate contains as little as 5% cocoa, the other ingredients are usually sugar, solid hydrogenated vegetable fats, nut oils, and a host of artificial flavourings. These types of fats are hidden in so many processed foods, and it is difficult to imagine that this kind of chocolate could possibly make a positive contribution to your health. The use of any fat other than cocoa butter is to my mind unacceptable. Cocoa butter occurs naturally in cocoa beans, and it has many qualities that make it a desirable commodity in its own right. The cosmetics and pharmaceutical industries buy tonnes of the stuff every year, to make into lipsticks, creams and suppositories, for which they are happy to pay a premium. It must be sorely tempting for industrial chocolate makers to remove the cocoa butter and sell it on, substituting it with other cheap and readily available hydrogenated fats. You may ask, 'What difference does it make anyway?' Firstly, you can feel the difference in the mouth – these 'trans fats' do not melt properly and leave a greasy coating on the palate. More importantly, perhaps, some hydrogenated fats have been linked with serious health problems, whereas cocoa butter acts to lower blood cholesterol levels.

looking for the real thing

Real chocolate can be hunted out easily enough – it is mostly a question of learning to read and interpret the wrappers. Look out for high cocoa content but there's no need to exaggerate; 50–70% cocoa solids are usually a good sign. I don't know anyone who drinks wine who would select a bottle using the alcohol content as a guide to quality. Normally the deciding factors would be the grape variety, appellation, vintage year, country of origin, as well as the colour.

A reliable indicator in recognizing real chocolate is the use of natural vanilla over vanillin (an artificial flavouring derived from pine trees). It is not that I am so against vanillin in itself, but it does seem to be a good marker to differentiate the sheep from the goats. The price of vanillin is almost negligible and hence it is used injudiciously, often with a view to masking the true nature of the cocoa beans in an inferior product. In spite of this general rule, there are plenty of examples of excellent chocolate where vanillin is used. Probably the best way of spotting a really fine chocolate is to find out about the origin and variety of the cocoa beans.

I have often heard people say, 'I don't like dark chocolate – it's bitter'. There are very few who, having tasted the real thing, still protest. The reality is that low-quality dark chocolate *is* often bitter, in spite of the high sugar content, because the cocoa beans used have been over-roasted and then, to compensate for their poor flavour, are padded out with sugar and (usually hydrogenated) fat. Real-chocolate makers select their cocoa beans very carefully; indeed, the similarity to wine making or coffee roasting comes to mind. Fine-flavoured varieties are carefully roasted to enhance the flavour. The process of refining the chocolate is a slow one, and extra cocoa butter is usually added to give the most sensuous silken texture when melting in the mouth.

I don't wish to dwell on the negative aspects of 'fast' chocolate, but it is essential you are able to differentiate between the two. This understanding might help to wean you off the sugar-high so commonly induced by this kind of confectionery. Once you have been initiated into the joys of really satisfying dark chocolate which hits the spot, the temptation to eat the 'fast' chocolate might just evaporate. Good dark chocolate contains 512 calories per 100g, so a 5g square (the perfect size I think) would have less than 26 calories. A small apple weighs 100g and has 46 calories.

the five senses chocolate test

Now you know the difference between 'real' and 'fast' chocolate, put your knowledge to the test with my unique Five Senses Chocolate Test. It's a fun thing to do with friends and will get you thinking about chocolate as never before. Start with four or five bars of dark chocolate, selecting ones with a range of cocoa solids content from 30–70%. Test the chocolate with 70% cocoa solids first, then move down the scale. You need to start with a clean palate, so have a drink of water. Too much sugar or salt interferes with the tasting, as do strong flavours like peppermint or chilli.

smell

We all know how when we have a cold food just seems to lose its flavour and everything tastes the same. That's because smell is without doubt the most finely tuned of all the five senses. So

the first thing to do is to sniff the chocolate and see what you can smell. Some of the aromas will remind you of intense fruit, wood, tobacco, caramel or even burnt rubber. Like a good wine, a good chocolate will have a well-balanced, pleasing smell.

sight

Next, break the bar of chocolate. When it's snapped, you can see a very characteristic texture in the break, a bit like tree bark. The other things to look for are the condition and colour of the chocolate. It should be glossy, without any bloom. A bloom indicates that it has been stored in damp or warm conditions. The colour of the chocolate will tell you about the type of cocoa used, and how highly roasted it is. In general, the redder the hue, the better the cocoa.

touch

Real chocolate should melt when held in the hand for a few seconds. The reason for this is that cocoa butter is solid and crystalline at 33°C, but melts at 34°C. The speed of melting is an indicator of what proportion of cocoa butter the chocolate contains: the higher the proportion, the better quality the chocolate, and the faster it melts.

sound

Break the chocolate next to your ear. Real chocolate has a distinctive snap caused by the cocoa butter crystals. 'Fast' chocolate is more like plasticine; expect a dull thud.

taste

At last you've reached the stage you've been waiting for. You may think that tasting the chocolate will give you the best idea of its quality, but what your tongue will also tell you, though, is how smooth the chocolate is, or in other words, the particle size. In real chocolate, this should be so fine that it will not be discernible. The taste test will also reveal the chocolate's finish. Real chocolate should linger deliciously in the mouth, like good wine. If there's any greasy residue, it means the chocolate contains fats other than cocoa butter. And finally, as the chocolate melts in the mouth, it releases volatile aromas … and we're back to smell again. Enjoy!

chocolate
know-how

masterclass:
ganache

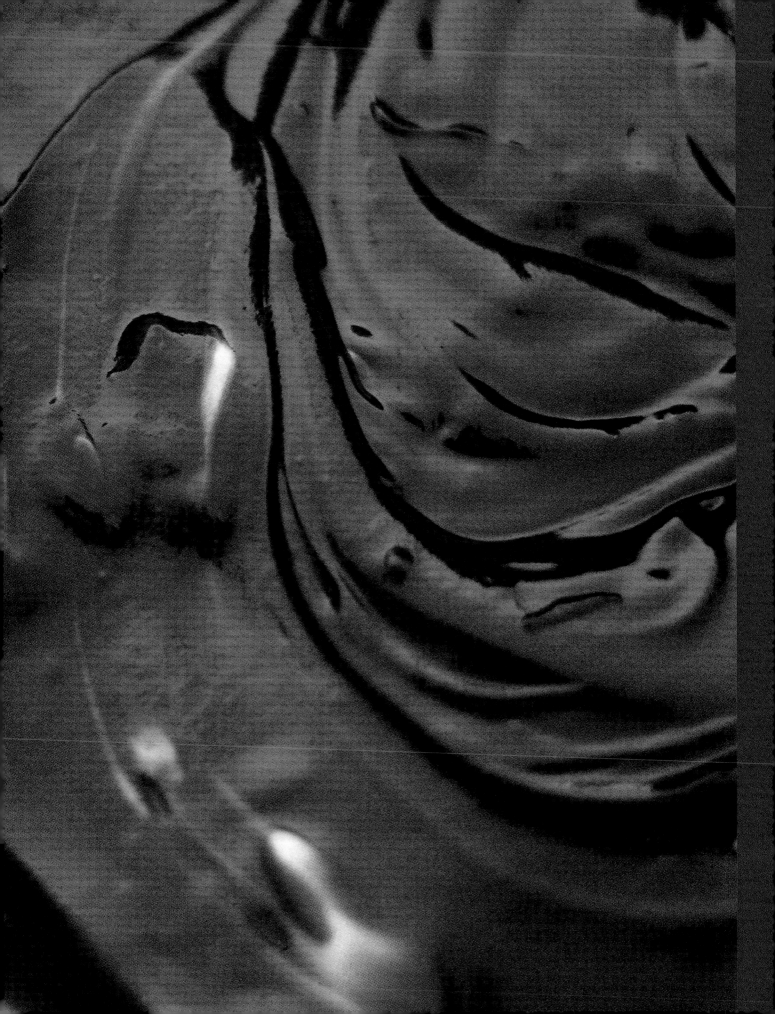

ganache

A ganache, otherwise known as a truffle, is one of the essential building blocks that will be used again and again in this book. Once mastered, it is simple and will revolutionize the way you cook with chocolate.

The basic ganache is an emulsion of chocolate, cream and butter. Some recipes will omit the butter when the finished result might be over-rich. You can also use custard instead of cream, as in the Pear and Chocolate Tart on page 130, for a lighter and healthier mixture. Sometimes you will use the 'raw' ganache, which will set to a stiff truffle texture when chilled, and other times the ganache will be cooked, as in the tart.

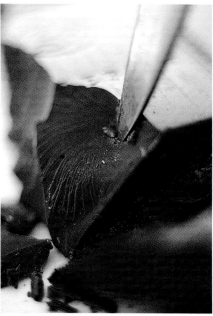

serves 6

500ml whipping cream
550g real dark chocolate
125g unsalted butter, diced

Always use the best chocolate you can (see Looking for the Real Thing on pages 23–5). Chop it into chunks or break it into squares. In a food processor, continue to chop the chocolate until it is a fine powder. It may actually just start to melt, but that's fine. If you have any big lumps, it might spoil your ganache. Put the chocolate into a heatproof bowl.

Scald the cream in a pan – allow it to boil and rise up (be careful it doesn't boil over). Pour about a tablespoon on to the chocolate and mix well. Keep adding the cream, a spoonful at a time, mixing it in thoroughly. This should ensure that you will achieve the perfect emulsion (the process is a bit like making mayonnaise).

When all the cream has been mixed in, add the butter. The mixture should still be warm enough to melt it, although it will take a few minutes to beat it in, so there are no lumps left. Do not be tempted to use pre-melted butter, as this will make a very heavy ganache.

water ganache

When I was initially told of a French *chocolatier* making water ganache, my first reaction was that it was impossible. A ganache is basically an emulsion of two fatty components, like egg yolks and oil in mayonnaise. A ganache of water and chocolate breaks all the rules of chocolate-making, as water and chocolate are sworn enemies (see page 25). I liked the idea of this challenge and decide to try it. The result was astonishing – it worked, and was 'creamy' in spite of there being no cream. It did not split and was eaten without hesitation by all my family. I use it for low-fat mousses and cakes. There is a version with tea, and it can also be made with coffee. Experiment and see what other ideas you can come up with.

serves 6

225g real dark chocolate (see pages 23–4)
225ml boiling water

cream or crème fraîche, to serve
(optional)

Break or chop the chocolate into pieces and melt in a low oven (see Melting chocolate below). When melted, make the ganache by adding the boiling water to the chocolate spoonful by spoonful. It will thicken quickly at first, but it should become a smooth mixture when all the water is mixed in (see making a ganache on page 30). Put into 6 small coffee cups or glasses and chill. Serve with cream or crème fraîche if you want.

melting chocolate

I never use a bain-marie – or even the traditional improvised bowl over a pan of hot water – to melt chocolate, as there is a danger that steam will get into the chocolate and ruin it. Much simpler is to use a very low oven (50-100°C) and put the chopped chocolate in a heatproof bowl. Leave in the oven for 5 minutes, then check with a fork; leave for another minute if it isn't all melted and test again. In the old days many chocolate makers used a box with a light bulb set under a bowl, and the chocolate was left to melt overnight.

tea ganache (vegan)

serves 6

225g real dark chocolate

1 heaped dsp fine perfumed China tea,
   like Earl Grey

225ml boiling water

touch of orange flower water (optional)

cream or crème fraîche, to serve
   (optional)

Break or chop the chocolate into pieces and melt in a low oven (see Melting chocolate, opposite). When melted, make the tea in a tea pot using the boiling water. Let it stand for 2 minutes, but it must not stew! Make the ganache by adding the tea to the chocolate spoonful by spoonful. It will thicken quickly at first, but it should become a smooth mixture when all the tea is mixed in (see making a ganache, page 30). Stir in the orange flower water, if using. Put into 6 small tea cups or glasses and chill for a few hours. Serve with cream or crème fraîche if you want.

plain and simple chocolate sauce

This is a simple recipe, using roughly one part water to two parts chocolate by weight.

200g real dark chocolate

100g water

Chop the chocolate. Boil the water in a heavy pan, then add the chocolate to the boiling water, whisking all the time, and being careful not to burn it. It should be a thick glossy sauce, with a perfectly smooth consistency. Serve with vanilla ice-cream or anything else.

variation

For a spicy chocolate sauce, stir in a pinch each of ground cardamom and ground chilli.

plain chocolate truffles

There are many ways to skin a cat…

With truffles, everyone has their own recipe and variations on the basic method: some whip the cream before adding it to pre-melted chocolate – I normally use very finely chopped chocolate which is melted by the boiling cream; some whisk the truffle mixture when it is finished to aerate it. Personally I prefer a dense, intense mixture, but it's a very personal thing.

Here are a few variations from some famous chocolate makers. Frederic Bau from Valrhona says that the chopped chocolate and boiled cream method gives the longest-lasting flavour, which is only really a consideration if you want to make these professionally.

Robert Linxe's recipe

(the high priest of chocolatiers, La Maison du Chocolat)
(makes about 75)

250g Valrhona Caraque
250g Valrhona extra bitter chocolate
300g whipping cream
more chocolate, to enrobe
unsweetened cocoa powder, to dust

Rococo recipe

(makes about 100)
(as in basic ganache, page 30)

550g real dark chocolate
500ml whipping cream
125g unsalted butter
unsweetened cocoa powder, to dust

Michel Chaudun's recipe

(makes about 100)

700g real dark chocolate
270g whipping cream
¼ vanilla pod
50g soft butter
200g unsweetened cocoa powder

Make a ganache with the chocolate and cream as described on page 30, infusing the vanilla if you are using it in the cream as you warm it. Leave to cool in a bowl or tray for about 15 minutes in the refrigerator, then beat in the butter and return to the refrigerator. When it has set to the consistency of butter icing, it is ready to be piped or spooned into truffle-sized pieces.

If piping, put the mixture into a piping bag and pipe blobs of mixture about the size of a large cherry (10-12g) on to a tray covered with greaseproof paper or cling film. Leave to cool for at least 2 hours, preferably 24.

To finish, you can dip in tempered chocolate (described in detail on page 45) using a dipping fork or your fingers, then drop into a large baking tray deeply filled with cocoa powder, roll briefly and leave to set. Shake off excess (don't worry, most of the cocoa powder can be reused).

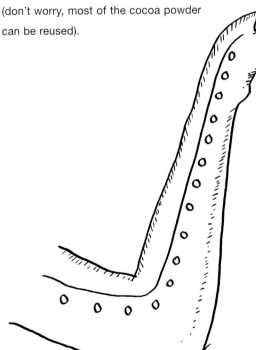

white chocolate, cardamom and saffron truffles

This recipe is one of the Rococo classics. I have always loved saffron, and when it is married with cardamom it has a particular resonance for me. The other great thing is that it takes the (sometimes rather sickly-sweet) edge off the white chocolate. If you don't like these flavours or would like to substitute another – feel free to experiment – try nutmeg or anything else you fancy.

makes about 100

500g real white chocolate
about 15 cardamom pods
375ml whipping cream
1 tsp ground saffron
225g unsalted softened butter

Chop the white chocolate finely in a blender or food processor.

Remove the outer skin from the cardamom pods and warm the seeds in a small pan, then crush them using a pestle and mortar.

Boil the cream with the saffron and cardamom for 2 minutes. Make a ganache with the chocolate and cream as described on page 30, adding the softened butter at the end. Pipe into blobs or scoop into truffle shapes with a spoon and leave to get really cool and solid.

Dip in tempered chocolate (see page 45), either white or dark. This can be tricky as the white chocolate makes the mixture rather soft and prone to melting as the truffles are dipped, so do it quickly and with a light hand.

variation
Finish by rolling them in chopped pistachio nuts instead of dipping them in chocolate.

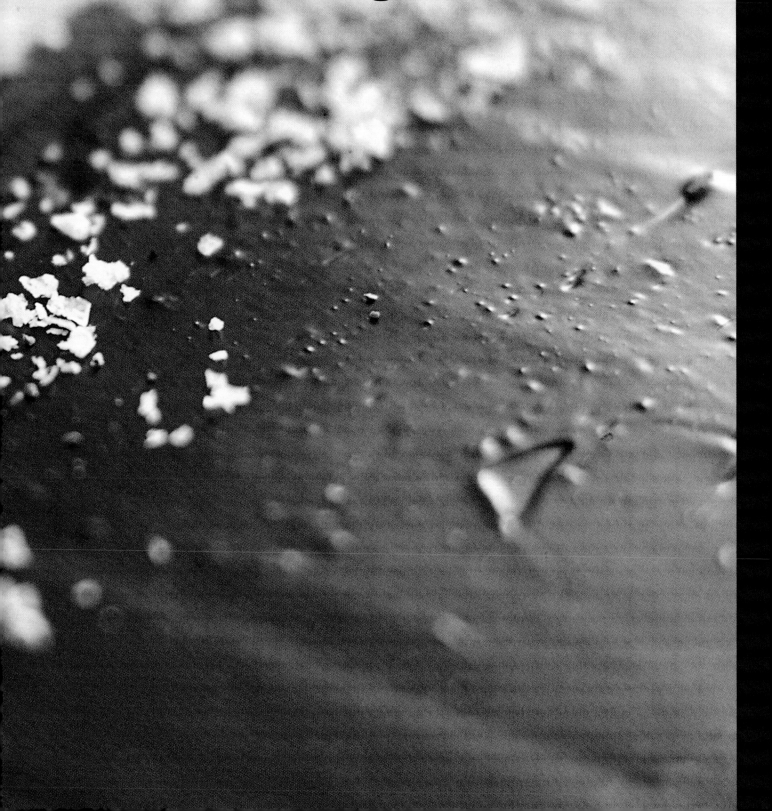

masterclass: tempering, moulding & sculpting

tempering chocolate

Tempering (also known as pre-crystallization) is probably the most frustrating aspect of chocolate making, until you understand how it works. The principles are really very simple, and once mastered it is a very straightforward procedure. It is a bit like learning to drive: the sort of thing that you have to do by yourself a few times until you have mastered the technique. There definitely is a technique. The good news is that you can re-temper chocolate over and over again, so long as it has been melted correctly and does not have a sugar or humidity bloom (see Storing chocolate on page 88).

When I was showing a class of five-year-olds how tempering is done, I used the example of the school children running around in the playground (melted chocolate, all the crystals elements dispersed), when the whistle is blown, and all the children form into orderly lines (or perfect chains of cocoa butter crystals in tempered chocolate). Cocoa butter is intrinsically unstable and by tempering chocolate, you are stabilizing it.

the reasons for tempering chocolate are to

1) give a beautiful gloss to moulded chocolate

2) help the chocolate shrink away from a mould and unmould perfectly

3) give the desired hardness and crystalline texture and crisp snap when broken

4) give stability to chocolate and help its keeping properties

5) prevent blooming (see page 88)

essential equipment:

1) As large a slab of marble as you can reasonably manage. The Rococo slab is about 1 metre by 2 metres, but a much smaller one will do. However, the bigger the slab the easier it is. At home, I have one small piece of marble, bought from IKEA, measuring 60 x 40cm. Tempering on it is really a bit fiddly, but it is possible.

2) A digital thermometer, which can be found in any serious catering shop and should not break the bank (around £10).

3) A large palette knife.

4) A triangular spreading knife/paddle/scraper - a large plasterer's filling knife from a DIY shop would be as good as anything, but it must be flexible.

5) Several stainless steel or Pyrex bowls.

let's get started!

1) Melt (decrystallize) as much chocolate as you need in a heatproof bowl. When it is completely fluid, and has no lumps in it. Check the temperature of the melted chocolate, it should be 55-58°C for dark chocolate, 45-50°C for milk chocolate and white chocolate.

2) Then pour three-quarters of it on to a cool, dry slab of marble. When I say cool this means not warmed by any bowls of chocolate, but not to be artificially cool, as this will cause the chocolate to crystallize too quickly. If that happens it will bloom and be difficult to work. Scrape chocolate remaining in the bowl down the sides so it doesn't cool too quickly.

3) Now, with the help of a paddle/scraper (the sort of large triangular blade used for DIY to fill holes with plaster), spread the chocolate over the marble. This will cool down the mass of chocolate and start to encourage the formation of the crystalline structure.

4) Then, holding the paddle in one hand and the palette knife in the other, quickly regroup the chocolate into the centre of the marble, being careful not to leave any trails behind, as they will cool too quickly. We are aiming to keep the temperature uniform as it cools. Repeat steps 3 and 4 a few times – notice how the chocolate begins to thicken.

5) Use the digital thermometer to check the temperature, but don't hang about as the chocolate is cooling all the time. When the dark chocolate has dropped to 28–29°C (milk chocolate 26–28°C, white chocolate 26–27°C) it is tempered and ready for the remaining melted chocolate to be added. (Be careful that it does not get too cool, you may be able to gently warm it but you might have to start all over again!) Many professional chocolatiers test the temperature by dipping their finger into the chocolate and then touching their bottom lip, as it is time-consuming checking the thermometer all the time, and, in fact, the lip is a very accurate gauge of temperature once you know what you are doing.

6) Now add the remaining melted chocolate. This will bring up the temperature by about 2°C, which is the final stage of the 'tempering curve' (melting, cooling, then raising the

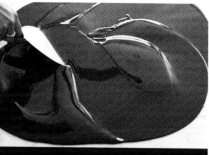

temperature slightly). Perfectly tempered chocolate has a very fine 'satin' sheen; if it has a dull finish, this is a sign that the chocolate has cooled too much and is not perfectly tempered.

7) Now the chocolate is ready to mould or dip truffles in. You need to be quite quick as the chocolate will lose its temper if it warms up or cools down. Transfer the tempered chocolate to a heatproof bowl. You can place the bowl of tempered chocolate in a bain-marie of lukewarm water (baby's bath temperature), which will help to keep it workable for longer.

Keep practising – after about 10 attempts you should be pretty good!

tips

A marble slab or other cool flat surface is essential. Work from one end of the marble to the other, and then back again so that the temperature of the marble remains stable. At the end don't be tempted to scrape off the hard bits from your palette knives as this will mess up your tempered chocolate – leave for consumption later, or give them to any willing helpers to lick. A stable room temperature of 20–24°C helps as does low humidity, less than 50 per cent. Different chocolates have different tempering curves. The precise temperatures vary with each chocolate. This is a technical point, and most manufacturers supply this information to anyone who needs it, as it is pretty important to get good results.

For most real dark chocolate, the starting temperature of the melted chocolate should not exceed 58°C. For milk or white chocolate, 50°C is the upper limit, because of the cassein, or milk protein, they contain. This protein is very sensitive to heat and will suddenly seize up at 54°C, rendering the chocolate useless.

Couverture is the technical name for the best-quality cooking chocolate, not to be confused with 'covering' chocolate which does not deserve to be called chocolate. Couverture must contain at least 31% cocoa butter. This rich chocolate is very fluid in its molten state and easy to work with, yet is very crisp and brittle when tempered.

chocolate curls or flakes or bark

Spread 150g warm, tempered chocolate (say using excess after making the trees later) on the slab with a palette knife until it's a couple of millimetres thick and the size of a piece of paper, say 23 x 30cm. Leave to set for a few minutes. You will get different results if the chocolate is set but not too hard or if it is still a bit soft, both are good – experiment. With the scraper, push the edge of the chocolate sheet hard and evenly, at an angle of about 45 degrees. You may get chocolate cigars, or it may crumple into flakes. If it's a disaster, melt the chocolate and start again.

chocolate leaves

These are easy and fun for children and adults alike. Experiment with different leaves. Those I find work best are reasonably thick but still flexible. Laurel and holly can be too stiff, and ivy and bamboo too flimsy. The surfaces of leaves vary too – some shiny, others flat. My favourites are hydrangea and camellia. Try a selection.

150g tempered chocolate

2 dozen leaves (see above)

You can paint either side of the leaf, but I do undersides, as the veining comes out best that way. Paint carefully. The important thing, especially if children are involved, is to try to keep the other sides clean. If there is chocolate on the wrong side it can cause the chocolate leaves to break when peeling them off. When dry, paint on another layer and then repeat again if you have the patience. Leave to set for 20 minutes or so, then carefully peel the real leaves off the chocolate ones.

dipped fruit

When you have mastered the art of tempering, temper about 150g chocolate of your choice. I find that white chocolate and strawberries work very well together, and dark chocolate is particularly good with cherries and cape gooseberries.

Pick really perfect fruit, and half dip it. Place the dipped fruit on greaseproof paper and refrigerate. You don't need to worry about condensation, as these will not be hanging around! Eat them as soon as they are ready, in about 10 minutes. You can also use nuts and candied peel, anything you want really.

choc-dipped truffles

To dip truffles, you need roughly the same amount of chocolate again as you used when making the ganache, although when tempering chocolate it is always easier to temper a large quantity and make a batch of different things that need it, such as the leaves, hearts and trees. If you temper the chocolate, the truffles will have a crisp shell which will contrast with the soft ganache filling. (You can also roll the truffles in cocoa, icing sugar, coconut or chopped nuts.)

If you want your truffles to last as long as possible, leave the dipping for 24 to 48 hours after you have made and shaped the truffles at a temperature of 12–15°C. This will give the ganache long enough to crystallize, and therefore it will not shrink away from the tempered chocolate shell and create air pockets that might encourage the growth of mould. Temper your chocolate as described on pages 41-2, then transfer it to a heatproof bowl and drop your truffles in one by one, removing them with a dipping fork or your fingers, and placing them in a bowl of cocoa powder (or whatever you've chosen to finish the truffles) or on to a plate covered with a sheet of cling film.

surprise christmas trees

This idea came from a customer at Rococo who wanted to send her nieces in America some cash for Christmas. I hope they ate the trees themselves, and did not give them away; each tree contained a roll of $50 dollar bills! You will need a two-piece polycarbonate mould with clips, available from good kitchen shops. There will be lots of extra chocolate, but don't worry as you can use it to make other things later.

100g melted white or milk chocolate for the decorations (optional)

1kg real dark chocolate

Prepare the mould by polishing the surface with cotton wool. The cleaner and shinier the better. The decorations are applied to the inside of the mould before it is filled rather than to the moulded object. Using the tempered white or milk chocolate, here's your chance to let your creative spirit loose. Either make a cone of greaseproof paper to pipe the decorations or use a small paint brush. Remember that everything will come out as a mirror image, so if you are writing you need to practise your mirror writing. You can prepare a template and place it under the mould as a guide, or just work free style. Also when making pairs, any decoration touching the sides needs to be matched on the pairing mould. Probably it is easiest to keep away from the edges, and then you won't have to worry about this. Don't be inhibited, try out different brush marks and vary the thickness of the white chocolate, you can get very fine detail. Leave the decorated moulds to dry at room temperature.

Temper your chocolate as described on pages 40–42 and put it in a bowl set over lukewarm water. Clip the sides of the tree together. Ladle the chocolate into the moulds, filling to the brim. Pour back the bulk into the bowl, tapping the mould with the scraper handle. Scrape off any excess from the rim, and invert the mould, so the chocolate pools in the tip. Leave for about 5 minutes, then check to see if the chocolate is drying. It may still look wet in places, which is fine. Repeat the process for a second layer, which should achieve the desired thickness. Place a small surprise wrapped in cellophane (money, jewellery or even a message or poem) into the mould, gently wedging it so it doesn't fall out when you invert the mould.

You now need to make a base for the tree. On a side-plate-sized piece of paper, make a puddle of tempered chocolate a bit bigger than the base of the tree. Press the open end of the mould into the puddle, releasing any trapped air bubbles, until it stands upright on the paper. Leave to harden for 15 minutes at room temperature, then put it in the fridge for half an hour. The time can vary depending on the thickness of chocolate and fridge temperature. Check at intervals until you see a halo where the tempered chocolate is contracting away from the mould. Then you need to take it out of the fridge; if you leave it too long, you might have problems with condensation. Peel off the paper and snap off the excess chocolate puddle, which should come away cleanly. If you can now bear to leave the tree in the mould for a few hours you should achieve a glossier object. When you come to unmoulding, release the clips and all tap the mould gently - the tree should just pop out...

variation

Love Hearts can be made in the same way, using the appropriate moulds.

real chocolate delight

savoury
chocolate

aubergine and tahini crostini

Well-cooked aubergines melt sweetly in the mouth in much the same way as really good chocolate; they are incredibly sensual vegetables. Many of us are put off them when they are badly prepared and either not cooked or bitter. The Middle Eastern repertoire understands how to treat them, perhaps better than anyone else does. This is one of my all-time favourite childhood treats, though at that time the chocolate was just a twinkle in my eye. This is the sort of recipe where the quantities need not be too precise, rather trust your taste buds and adjust the flavours as you see fit.

makes 24 bite-sized pieces

1 large or 2 small aubergine(s)

4 tbsp tahini (sesame paste)

juice of 1–2 lemon(s)

2 garlic cloves, chopped

1 dsp unsweetened cocoa powder

large pinch of sea salt

French baguette or Italian ciabatta, for the crostini

handful of roughly chopped flat-leaf parsley, to garnish (optional)

sprinkling of smoked paprika (optional)

extra-virgin olive oil, for dressing (optional)

Ideally, the aubergines should be cooked whole, slowly over charcoal, but failing that they can be scorched over a naked gas flame, or roasted in the oven at its hottest setting for 20 minutes, until blackened and collapsed. Leave to cool.

Peel off the skin, reserving any of the flavourful juices, and pulse flesh and juices with the tahini, lemon juice, garlic, cocoa and salt until you have a smooth paste. You may need to add more lemon juice or a bit of water if it seems too thick, this depends on the tahini, which can vary from being almost liquid to a fairly solid peanut-butter consistency.

Preheat the oven to 180°C/Gas 4. Slice the bread thinly at an angle to produce good crostini shapes, place on a baking tray and bake until crisp and golden. Let cool on a wire rack. Just before serving, spread the tapenade on the toasts and finish with a little parsley and paprika, if you like. You can also dress them with a few drops of good olive oil.

Beetroot and tahini crostini

This is very much the same as the Aubergine and Tahini Crostini on the previous page, substituting freshly cooked (not in vinegar) beetroot for the aubergine. It is the most dramatic shade of deep pink, almost purple, when blended with the tahini. The sweet yet earthy flavour of this much maligned root vegetable is set off by the other ingredients, and the colour set alight by a dribble of green extra-virgin olive oil and some flat-leaf parsley.

crostini with goats' cheese and chocolate tapenade

This recipe has been made many times and shared with friends and colleagues around the world. It is based on the Claudia Roden's olive toasts – classic Mediterranean antipasti. I don't normally tell anyone about the chocolate until they have tasted these crostini, as it is hard to discern the flavour, but it definitely adds something.

Makes about 30 pieces

25g real dark chocolate, melted

150g pitted ripe black olives (buy 300g if you are pitting them yourself)

5 preserved anchovy fillets, drained and chopped

1 large garlic clove, chopped

2 tbsp capers, drained and excess vinegar squeezed out

5 tbsp good-quality extra-virgin olive oil

2 tbsp rum (optional)

some chopped fresh chilli (optional)

French baguette or Italian ciabatta, for toast

225g fresh soft goats' cheese

cayenne pepper, for sprinkling

a few sprigs of parsley or dill (optional)

Put all the ingredients except the bread, goats' cheese, cayenne pepper and herbs in the food processor and pulse them until everything is mixed, but still retains some texture. Make the toasts as described on the previous page and allow to cool on a wire rack. Just before serving, spread the tapenade on the toasts, then place a thin slice of goats' cheese on top and finish with a sprinkle of cayenne pepper and a herb leaf.

chocolate sushi

This recipe was presented at a chocolate masterclass given at the Eurochoc Festival in Perugia. I assisted *chef chocolatier* Paul de Bondt and chef Alessandro Battistero, and the sushi uses my chocolate tapenade in its centre. Making sushi looks quite daunting first time round, but it's actually very simple. The sushi vinegar, nori, umeboshi, wasabi, pickled vinegar and sushi mat can all be found in specialist Japanese shops, some health food stores and many better supermarkets or department-store food halls. If you can't find ready-toasted nori you can toast it yourself lightly over a gas burner. The accompanying Salt and Pepper Chocolate can be made well in advance if you prefer.

makes 24 pieces

275g Japanese rice

6 tbsp sushi vinegar, plus more for the hands

4 large sheets of toasted nori seaweed

12 drained canned anchovy fillets

½ cucumber, peeled, halved, deseeded and cut into long strips

8 umeboshi plums, quartered, stoned and cut into strips, or 4 tbsp umeboshi paste (optional)

for the chocolate tapenade

150g pitted black olives (these taste much better if you choose big juicy kalamata olives and pit them yourself; if you can't be bothered, use tinned pitted olives)

1 garlic clove, roughly chopped

2 tbsp capers, drained and roughly chopped

30g melted real dark chocolate

for the salt and pepper chocolate

200g tempered chocolate (pages 40-41)

scant tsp flaky sea salt

scant tsp cracked black pepper

to serve

wasabi (Japanese horseradish)

pickled ginger

for the dipping sauce

4 tbsp light soy sauce

1 tbsp dry sherry or mirin (Japanese rice wine)

First prepare the rice: soak it in cold water for 10 minutes, drain off excess water, put the rice into a heavy pan and add 350ml fresh cold water. Bring to the boil, turn down the heat and simmer, covered, for 6–7 minutes until just tender and all the water has been absorbed. Fluff up the rice and place in a large flat dish or baking tray.

Add the sushi vinegar and mix well with a spatula, while fanning the rice to cool it quickly. (In Japanese sushi kitchens, they have someone whose job it is just to fan the rice!) When cool, put to one side.

Prepare the tapenade by processing all the ingredients together to make a rough paste.

To assemble the sushi: first place a sheet of toasted nori shiny side down on a bamboo sushi mat. With vinegared hands, spread a quarter of the rice evenly over the entire width and two-thirds of the depth of the nori. Arrange a line of anchovies and tapenade along the middle of the rice across the width and put the cucumber strips on top together with the umeboshi plums or purée if using.

Using the mat, roll up the nori to make a cylinder about 4cm in diameter, then press it in the rolled mat to form it into a square shape. Repeat with the other pieces of nori and remaining ingredients. Using a sharp knife, cut each length in half, then cut each of these into 3 pieces.

To make the Salt and Pepper Chocolate: spread the tempered chocolate as thinly as possible on a sheet of cellophane (if you can't find any, a tray covered in cling film will do, but make sure it won't slip about). Try to sprinkle the salt and pepper as evenly over the surface of the chocolate as possible. When it has started to cool, divide it into squares about 3 x 4 cm and leave on the sheet to finish cooling in the fridge for 10 minutes.

Arrange the pieces of sushi carefully on a serving dish and spear each with a piece of Salt and Pepper Chocolate. Serve with a small mountain of wasabi, some pickled ginger and the dipping sauce made by mixing the soy sauce and sherry or mirin.

chocolate tempura

Well-made and really freshly served tempura is a rare treat. It is possible to make it in a domestic kitchen, but always use fresh oil and cook the tempura in very small batches to keep the oil at the right temperature. An electric deep-fryer is a great help, but you can use a wok or deep heavy pan. Serve each batch immediately and carry on cooking! You can batter and deep-fry almost anything, from Mars Bars to boiled quails' eggs. Choose whatever you want, but don't just cook one thing; a selection of four or five is best. The basic batter recipe comes from Madhur Jaffrey's *Eastern Vegetarian Cooking*. Cocoa nibs are the raw material from which chocolate is made, they come from the whole beans which have been nibbed or cracked. Very nutty, they give great texture to savoury dishes.

serves 4

20 string beans

8 baby artichokes, quartered

2 red peppers

8 asparagus spears

2 sweet potatoes

8 baby aubergines

thin end of a butternut squash, peeled
   and thinly sliced

8 whole spring onions

200g tofu, cut into strips

12 shelled and deveined raw king prawns

1 medium-sized squid, cleaned and cut
   into rings

225g raw tuna, cut into chunks

grapeseed, groundnut or sunflower oil,
   for deep-frying

for the dipping sauce

1 tbsp soy sauce

4 tbsp sake or mirin

2 tbsp Chocolate Balsamic Vinegar
   (page 60)

150ml dashi or good-quality vegetable
   stock or dried mushroom soaking water

2 tbsp grated fresh ginger

225g grated daikon (mooli)

for the batter

1 egg yolk

450ml ice-cold water

200g plain flour

60g cocoa nibs (see above)

handful of chopped fresh coriander

1-2 small fresh chilli(es), deseeded and
   chopped, or more to taste

to serve

tube of ready-made wasabi

First, start the sauce: mix together the soy sauce, sake or mirin, vinegar and dashi.

Prepare the batter by beating the egg yolk in a bowl until smooth, then beat in the iced water. Finally, add the flour, cocoa nibs, coriander and chilli. Beat briefly, but the mixture should still be lumpy (if you over-mix, it will be tough when cooked)! Leave to stand for 10 minutes, while you heat the oil in a wok or deep-fryer.

Meanwhile, prepare any vegetables that are too large to cook whole, slicing them into very even slices so that they all cook at the same rate. Flour any wet ingredients before dipping them into the batter. Heat the oil until just beginning to smoke (190°C). Fry small batches of one sort of vegetable/fish at a time. Drain on kitchen paper before serving.

Mix ginger and daikon into the dipping sauce and serve this and wasabi with the tempura.

chocolate balsamic vinegar

I have found this little invention totally invaluable. As well as its obvious uses, say in salad dressings and deglazing pans to make gravies and sauces, you will see it delivers the chocolate element in lots of my savoury recipes. It does, though, also lend itself to dishes other than savoury – just try it over fresh strawberries. For a more piquant version to use with red meat and cheese dishes, like Welsh rabbit, add 100ml Worcestershire sauce.

Makes about 225ml

100g white caster sugar

100ml vinegar (I used equal parts cider and cooking balsamic)

30g grated real dark chocolate

Gently heat the sugar and vinegar in a small deep pan until all the sugar has dissolved, then allow to bubble gently for 5 minutes.

Take off the heat, whisk in the chocolate well and leave to cool. When cool, stir again quickly. Pour into a small clean jam jar to store until needed.

james's 5-minute chocolate devilled kidneys

This is one of my husband's favourite dishes, which was in the Booth family repertoire before he was born. I let him make it because I hate cutting up kidneys. In fact, I would have sworn that I hated kidneys until he made me taste these (the same recipe sans chocolate). When James was a small boy, his father would be served this dish for supper as a special treat, while all the boys waited on the side lines for a 'bonus'. James's mother cooks them for about half an hour, but I think, like squid, they can be flash-fried in a wok in a couple of minutes and be just as good – if not better.

serves 2

6–8 very fresh lamb kidneys (preferably organic)

1 dsp Dijon mustard

1 tbsp tomato paste

1 dsp oyster sauce

1 glass of dry sherry, sake or red wine

1 tsp anchovy essence

2 tbsp grapeseed oil, olive oil or any light vegetable oil

1 onion, chopped

1 or 2 garlic cloves, thinly sliced

1 dsp unsweetened cocoa powder

black pepper or chilli, to taste

to serve

steamed basmati or Thai rice, or toast

crème fraîche (optional)

handful of flat-leaf parsley

Prepare the kidneys by halving them and removing the white core very carefully. Make a sauce of all the wet ingredients except the oil.

Heat the oil in a wok and quickly cook the onions and garlic; put to one side. Flash-fry the kidneys for 2 minutes, then return the onions to the pan, together with the sauce, cocoa and pepper or chilli to taste. Cook until the sauce is bubbling and the consistency of single cream. If too thick, add more wine – the rice will absorb the sauce, so you'll need plenty.

Serve with steamed basmati or Thai rice. Add a dollop of crème fraîche, if you like, and some flat-leaf parsley. Alternatively, the kidneys are also delicious on toast as an after-dinner savoury or for breakfast. If you can't stand kidneys, use big mushrooms instead.

green henry

This recipe is a traditional Northern German recipe, made by my old friend Ariane Severin. I enjoyed it very much, and thought it a suitable case for a chocolate spin. Normally made in the summer, with freshly picked beans and under-ripe pears, serve it as a dish on its own or as a vegetable accompaniment to meat, fowl, game or sausages.

serves 4-6

500g bacon or pancetta in a piece, cut into rough cubes

1 tbsp olive oil

15g butter

1kg freshly picked green beans (string or haricot)

500g small unripe pears, skins left on

1 glass of red wine

2 tbsp balsamic vinegar

salt and pepper

25g real dark chocolate, finely chopped

freshly grated nutmeg

handful of chopped parsley

Fry the bacon or pancetta in a little oil and butter until well cooked and then remove any excess fat from the pan. Remove the tops from beans, but there's no need to take off the tails. Put the beans and the whole pears on top of the bacon, cover with 500ml water and the wine and vinegar, but do not stir. Cover the pan with a lid and leave to simmer for about 40 minutes, or until the pears are cooked through.

To serve, arrange a pile of beans and bacon on each plate and top with a whole pear. Boil the sauce in the pan to reduce by about half, season with pepper and add the chocolate. Pour some of the sauce over each pear and sprinkle the beans with a grating of nutmeg and some parsley.

hangover fried eggs

This quick dish is perfect at any time of the day or night – and is especially good for chasing away hangovers! Put a knob of butter in a frying pan. When sizzling and starting to blacken at the edges, put one or two eggs into the pan, sprinkle with salt and pepper, and cook to taste – I like mine easy over (turned over and cooked briefly on the other side). Put the eggs on a warm plate and deglaze the pan with a tablespoon of Chocolate Balsamic Vinegar (page 60). Crusty bread and salad turn it into a more substantial dish.

james's real guacamole

My husband James travelled in Mexico as a student and declares no one knows how to make 'real' guacamole. In this, garlic, cream cheese, sour cream and other spurious ingredients are banned. It is actually very easy and delicious. Possibly a little chopped fresh coriander would be permissible. There's no chocolate in this recipe! It is, however, the perfect foil to the beans on page 81, and a great addition to any of the other chocolate mezze.

serves 4

2 ripe avocados

juice of 1 lemon or 2 limes

2 ripe tomatoes, blanched in boiling water and skinned

½ red onion, very finely chopped

really good pinch of sea salt

½ small red fresh chilli, deseeded and finely chopped, or ground chilli to taste

Scoop the flesh out of the avocados, keeping the stones, and put into a bowl. Cover with lemon or lime juice and mash lightly with a fork – it doesn't need to be a smooth purée.

Skin the tomatoes, squeeze out and discard the seeds and juice. Remove any hard or pithy bits of flesh and chop finely. Mix this, the onion, salt and chilli into the avocado. If you don't want to eat this immediately, put the stones back into the guacamole and chill in the fridge. This stops the mixture from going brown. Remove and stir before serving.

aubergine, chocolate and goats' cheese pizzette

The aubergine mixture is based on the Sicilian caponata, and uses sweet-and-sour elements of vinegar and chocolate to complement the aubergine. The pizza and goats' cheese are among my all-time favourite ingredients.

These baby pizzas can be assembled and cooked at the last minute, having prepared all the ingredients beforehand, making them perfect finger food. Make the dough 6–8 hours ahead: in the morning or the night before, if you are having this for lunch.

If you haven't got the time to make the Chocolate Balsamic Vinegar, or don't want to be bothered, you could sprinkle the cooked aubergine with some unsweetened cocoa powder and balsamic vinegar before assembling the pizza.

Makes about 8-10 small pizzette

for the pizza dough
400g 00 (Italian doppio zero) flour

8g sugar

12g dried yeast

8g salt

250ml iced water

for the topping
2 aubergines, each about 350g

1 big red onion, finely chopped

2 garlic cloves, finely chopped

½ fennel bulb, finely chopped

1 tbsp olive oil, plus more for the
  aubergine

15g butter

6 tomatoes, skinned, or 1 large tin of
  peeled plum tomatoes

semolina or plain flour, for dusting

200g fresh goats' cheese

handful of good black olives, pitted
  and halved

2 tbsp miniature capers

200g grated Cheddar, chopped
  mozzarella or other cheese

100g pine nuts

about 3 tsp Chocolate Balsamic Vinegar
  (page 60)

handful of chopped flat-leaf parsley

sprinkling of smoked paprika (optional)

Make the dough: in a large bowl, mix the flour with the sugar, yeast and salt, trying not to let them come into direct contact. Add some iced water and knead quickly, adding more

water as necessary, until you have a ball of elastic dough – this takes about 5 minutes. Cover the dough with cling film and put it into the fridge immediately. Leave it for an hour or two. This way of making the dough allows the yeast and flavours to develop very slowly, and when you roll it out it will burst into life.

Prepare the topping: cut the aubergines into quarters lengthwise, and then into 1cm slices. Salt the slices and leave to sweat in a colander.

Meanwhile, sauté the finely chopped onion, garlic and fennel in olive oil and butter over a low heat for 10–15 minutes. Add the tomatoes with their liquid and simmer for another 10–15 minutes, until it has a thickish, sauce-like consistency.

The aubergine will now be discoloured and covered in droplets of moisture. Pat the aubergine dry with kitchen towel and then shallow-fry in as little olive oil as possible in a large frying pan, until browned on both sides and quite well cooked, about 5 minutes. You may need to do this in batches.

Preheat the oven to the hottest temperature available. Oil several flat baking sheets then dust them with semolina. Whiz the tomato sauce with a hand-held mixer. Get the dough out of the fridge and cut it into 8–10 pieces. Roll each piece out as thinly as possible into 15cm rounds and arrange on the prepared baking trays. (You could even make miniature ones in tartlet tins.) Cover the pizzas with tomato sauce and arrange the aubergine, crumbled goats' cheese, olives and capers on top. Sprinkle with grated cheese and pine nuts, and put into the hot oven for 10–15 minutes until crisp.

Just before serving, drizzle the chocolate vinegar over the pizzette, followed by some flat-leaf parsley and smoked paprika if you like.

reverend mother's arm

At school we used to be given a steamed roly-poly suet pudding with jam in the middle which we took to calling 'Reverend Mother's arm'! I have used this idea to make a savoury pasta roll – to which you can give your own name!

In the past, I have made it for 30 people, but you need a large kitchen and big fish kettles to work on that scale. The advantage of making this roll over stuffing ravioli is that there is no danger of losing the filling when the ravioli explode, which does seem to happen, even for the most experienced of old pasta hands. You can also bake this roll in the oven, covered with a béchamel sauce.

Feel free to experiment with different fillings – roast pumpkin also works very well – and you can have up to four sorts of filling, depending on how elaborate you want it to be!

serves 8

for the pasta

> 200g 00 (Italian doppio zero) flour
>
> 1 tbsp unsweetened cocoa powder
>
> 2 fresh eggs (newly laid if possible)
>
> a very little ice-cold water
>
> about 30g cocoa nibs (page 59)

for the mushroom filling

> 50g dried porcini (cep), soaked in boiling
>
>   water to cover and left for an hour
>
> 1 small red onion, chopped
>
> 15g butter
>
> 1 tbsp olive oil
>
> 225g chestnut mushrooms, roughly
>
>   chopped
>
> salt and pepper

for the spinach and ricotta filling

> 500g spinach
>
> 125g ricotta cheese
>
> 125g crumbly blue cheese, like Stilton,
>
>   crumbled
>
> freshly grated nutmeg

for the beetroot and goats' cheese filling

> about 500g raw or cooked (as long as
>
>   not vinegared) beetroot
>
> 125g ricotta cheese
>
> 125g goats' cheese

to serve

> 100g toasted pine nuts, to garnish
>
> 225g unsalted butter
>
> big handful of fresh sage leaves

Make the pasta: sift the flour and cocoa powder into a food processor, then add the eggs, and blend to a smooth ball of dough (if too dry, add a little ice-cold water). You can also make and knead this dough by hand. Wrap in cling film and chill while you make the fillings.

To make the mushroom filling: first drain the porcini, reserving the liquid, squeeze out excess liquid and chop into pieces. Sauté the red onion in the butter and olive oil over a very low heat for about 15 minutes – don't to let it brown or burn. Add the porcini and fresh mushrooms, and cook for another 5 minutes. If they start to get too dry at any point, add some of the strained porcini soaking water. Season and allow to cool.

To make the spinach and ricotta filling: first cook the spinach for 2–3 minutes, either by steaming it or blanching it in boiling water. Drain, squeeze out as much water as possible and chop roughly. Mix it with the cheeses. Season to taste with salt, pepper and nutmeg.

To make the beetroot and goats' cheese filling: you can use ready-cooked beetroot as long as it was not cooked in vinegar, or cook your own. Do not pierce the beets, but test to see if they are cooked by trying to peel back the skin with your thumb – if you can, it is cooked. Leave to cool and then peel. Chop roughly, mix with the cheeses and seasoning.

To assemble the 'arm', if using a pasta machine, cut the dough into several equal-sized pieces. If you don't have a machine, roll the entire ball of dough by hand into a very smooth large rectangle as thin as possible (about 1mm). If making by machine, the strips need to be 'welded' together using a little water, again until you have a sheet about 30 x 45cm. The seams should be at right angles to the rolling edge, or the 'arm' may come apart.

Carefully place it on a clean old tea towel. Scatter the cocoa nibs over it and then spread the different mixtures evenly in stripes across it, leaving a blank strip about 5cm wide at the end and sides to seal. Start by rolling the filled end, using the towel to help if necessary. When rolled up, seal side and ends by dampening the edges with cold water and pressing firmly. Roll up in the towel and tie with string, so it looks like a fillet of beef.

To cook, immerse in boiling salted water and simmer for 30 minutes. Meanwhile, toast the pine nuts gently until golden. Make a sage butter by melting the butter in a pan, dropping in the sage and cooking for a few minutes. To serve, untie the bundle and cut into slices (ideally 2 per person), discarding ends. Serve with the sage butter and toasted pine nuts.

quick pan-roasted chicken with chocolate vinegar

One of my 'black beasts' is fast food, meaning the kind of stuff peddled to children on every shopping street in the developed world. It makes me angry on many counts, the cynical exploitation of children as a target audience, the apparent inability of parents to resist 'pester power', the nutritional paucity of the offering, and then the exploitation of cheap labour and cheaply raised factory-farmed animals*. This is my attempt to win my small children over with my version, and pander to their love of vinegar!

First, find a happily raised chicken, preferably organic or free-range, jointed. In a non-stick pan, blast the chicken for 5 minutes on each side, until well browned. Pour off any fat and season with salt, pepper and some fines herbes and garlic if they like it. Cover with a lid and continue to cook until the pieces are thoroughly cooked (about 10 more minutes, i.e. 20 minutes in all). Remove the chicken pieces and allow to rest for a few minutes. Collect any juices that have run from them (these should be clear – if pink, the chicken is not cooked through). De-glaze the pan with Chocolate Balsamic Vinegar (page 60) and the juices. Pour this sauce over the chicken. Serve with rice and a salad.

*I heartily recommend anyone interested in these issues to read *Fast Food Nation* by Eric Schlosser (Houghton Mifflin, 2001, ISBN 0-713-99602-1), which is a compelling read and very scary.

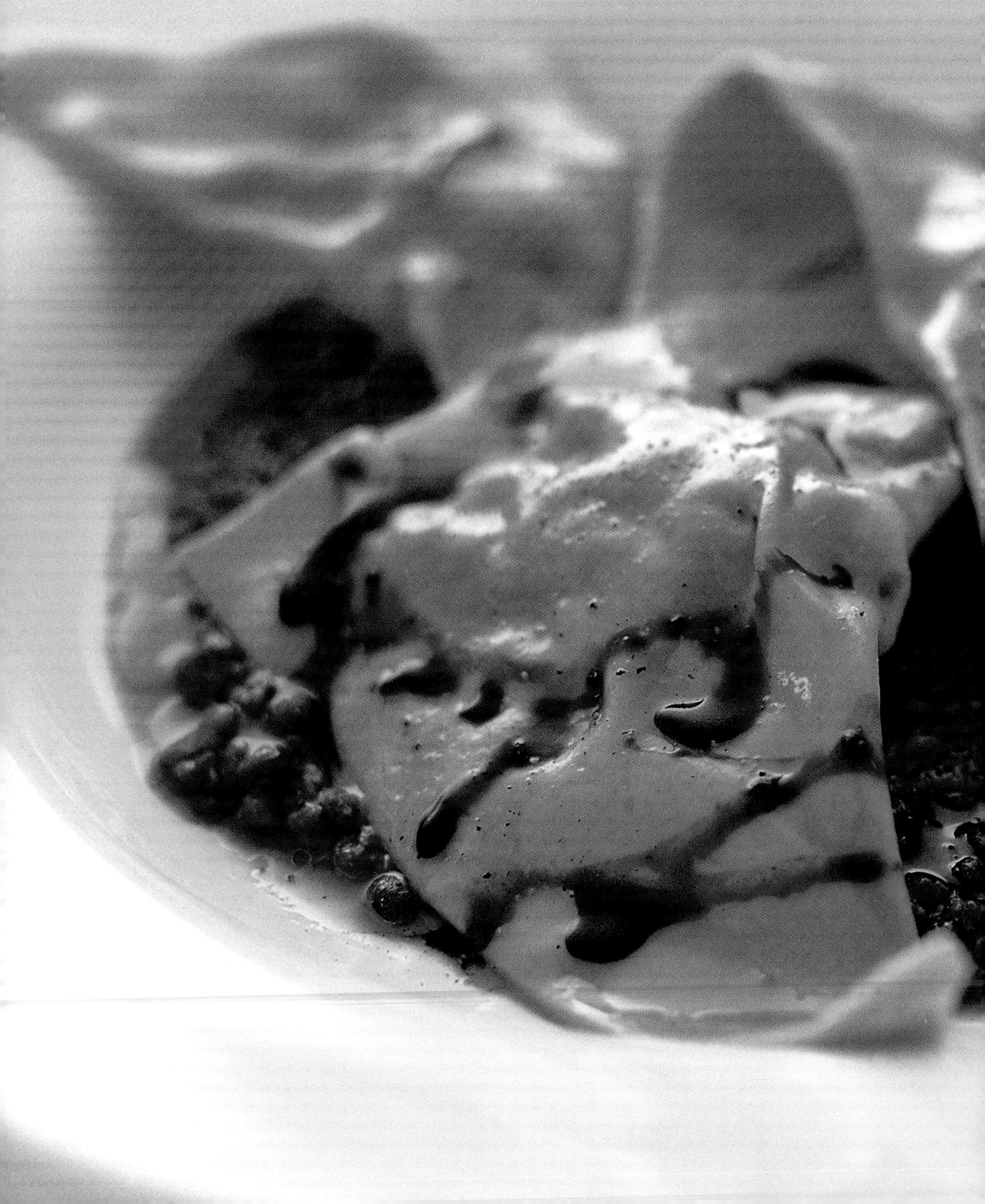

paul de bondt's mignon di pasta ripieni con passate di lentichhie (lentil puree with raviolini)

serves 8-10 as a first course

for the lentil purée

200g brown lentils (ideally Castellucci)

1 onion, very finely chopped

2 garlic cloves, very finely chopped

1 carrot, very finely chopped

½ celery stalk or small fennel bulb, very
finely chopped

1 tbsp olive oil

1 tbsp ras el hanout spices (optional)

small handful of fresh sage

small sprig of rosemary

2 bay leaves

for the pasta

3 large very fresh eggs, plus 1 extra yolk

salt

500g 00 (Italian doppio zero) flour

½ tbsp olive oil, plus more for drizzling

coarse semolina, for dusting

Chocolate Balsamic Vinegar (page 60),
for drizzling

for the stuffing

150g bread

250g lean pork fillet

250g sausage meat

30g toasted and ground hazelnuts

40g cocoa nibs (page 59)

salt and pepper

First make the lentil purée (this tastes best when made earlier): soften the chopped vegetables in olive oil over a very low heat until golden (about 10 minutes), but do not let them brown. Add the ras el hanout and fry for a minute. Cover with water (about twice the volume of the lentils) and bring to a simmer. Add the herbs and cook for 20 minutes to 1 hour, checking regularly to ensure the lentils are al dente. When cooked, strain off any excess water and reserve. Remove the herbs, divide the lentils in two and purée one half. Add to the whole lentils, bring to the boil, set aside and allow to cool. Adjust seasoning to taste and adjust its thickness with the reserved lentil water – it should be denser than soup.

Make the pasta dough: put the eggs, salt, flour and oil into the food processor and blend into a ball of dough. It should be rather stiff, though you can add a little water if you need to. Wrap in cling film and set aside to allow to rest while you make the stuffing.

Prepare the stuffing: soak the bread in water and squeeze dry. Mince this and all the other stuffing ingredients, except the cocoa nibs, in a food processor until roughly chopped. Break up the cocoa nibs with a rolling pin and mix into the meat. Season to taste.

Either by hand or with a pasta machine, roll the pasta into very thin sheets. Lydia Sodani, a superwoman married to a farmer with a Parmesan herd in Reggio Emilia, showed me how to make ravioli. The texture needs to be silky smooth, and you can only achieve this by repeated rolling. On the machine, I put it through about 6 or 7 times on the widest setting until very smooth. Between each passing, fold the sheet into as neat a rectangle as you can to ensure a regular shape that's then easy to work on the second smallest to get the final sheet. You may need extra flour to stop the dough sticking. When you have made your sheets, cut into 10–12cm squares. Place a spoonful of stuffing into the centre of each, seal the edges using a damp pastry brush (don't over-wet!), fold corner to corner and press down firmly to create a triangle. Trim the edge if necessary. Sprinkle a tray with coarse semolina and place them on it. They can be made a few hours ahead. There should be 3 per person.

Cook the ravioli in lots of gently boiling salted water, until the pasta is al dente, about 20 minutes – test by cutting off a bit of border. Some people say 4 minutes, but Lydia always cooked hers for much longer, usually 20, and so do I – it depends how thick the pasta is. Start testing from about 10 minutes. Take out of the pan individually and drain in a colander. Place in a warm frying pan with some olive oil and gently toss until gleaming. Serve 3 per portion on top of a mound of reheated lentil purée. Finish with a drizzle of oil and vinegar.

lacquered duck in chocolate sauce

This is Paul de Bondt's recipe, which he demonstrated in his chocolate masterclass during the Eurochocolate Festival in Perugia in 2000. I was guest chef part of the time, when I was not being commandeered to do tutored chocolate tastings with the delegates of the 'chocohouse' school in another part of the building. Paul began as a chef in Holland, and then fell in love with Italy, the Italians and one in particular, Cecilia Iacobelli. Between them they now own and run one of the very finest artisan chocolate shops in Italy.

Paul is full of energy and good ideas; he loves to brainstorm and shares his knowledge and enthusiasm of food, wine and chocolate with fellow professionals in a spirit which I find so refreshing. I have spent many inspiring hours in his company. Paul and Cecilia often prepare chocolate banquets and this is one of the dishes they might serve, although it needs plenty of time and planning in the preparation. My chocolate tapenade often features too (see Chocolate Sushi on page 55). Good accompaniments for the duck include: marinated ginger (bought), mixed with pieces of orange, orange juice and cooked orange peel cut in julienne strips, then served ice-cold in small bowls; fried soya noodles; onions and courgettes, stir-fried in a wok; curly raw leeks, all finished with toasted black and white sesame seeds.

serves 8

1 fine fresh duck, weighing about 1.5kg

50g sugar

50g honey

big lump of ginger, peeled and sliced into
   little strips

12 whole cardamom pods

a little liquorice root or powder (optional)

for the sauce

giblets, neck and wing tips of the duck

2 tbsp oil

1 onion, roughly chopped

1 celery stalk, roughly chopped

1 carrot, roughly chopped

1 tbsp soy sauce

small glass of dry sherry

30g unsweetened chocolate or very dark
   chocolate

cornflour (optional)

To prepare the duck, make a small hole in skin and blow up the poor beast with a compressor or a drinking straw. This lifts the skin, so that the fat underneath will drain out when cooking and the skin will become beautifully crisp. Cut off the neck and wing tips.

Make a thick syrup by boiling the sugar, honey and 300ml water together. Then add the ginger and cardamom, together with a little liquorice if you can find it! Paint the syrup on the duck and hang it in a cool, airy place (not the fridge) until the end of the day. Keep painting it with the syrup whenever you think about it.

Preheat the oven to 180°C/Gas 4. Place the duck on a rack over a roasting tin filled with water. Cook the duck until it is well roasted and caramelized, about 1½-2 hours.

To make the sauce, brown the duck neck and wings in a little oil, then add the onion, celery and carrots, and fry gently for a few minutes. Make a stock by adding the giblets, together with the ginger and cardamom taken from the sugar syrup and 300ml water. Boil for several hours until it has reduced by half, strain off and skim any fat from the top. Now add the soy sauce, dry sherry and finally the unsweetened or very dark chocolate to taste. This is the most critical part of the recipe – add the chocolate little by little and stop when you can discern the bitterness. If it needs to be thickened, add a little cornflour mixed with cold water, and boil until the sauce is no longer cloudy.

hare and chocolate sauce

Hare and chocolate are inextricably linked for me, as some of the most beautiful Easter moulds depict hares. Long before the Christian feast of Easter existed, the Roman dawn goddess Oestre was a symbol of new life and spring. She was said to disguise herself as a hare, and go around hiding eggs behind bushes – hence Easter-egg hunts.

Quite apart from that, the meat of the hare goes exceptionally well with chocolate. It is very dark, extremely lean and needs long cooking. I have tried several ways of cooking hare, and the best, in my opinion, is to make a ragu with it, to be served with tagliatelle. It is far superior to beef. My son, aged five, pronounced it delicious and said he'd like to eat it for supper every night. This recipe is an Italian classic and different versions can be found in many books; this one is probably closest to that served at the River Café. Making a change from spring lamb at Easter time, the chocolate gives body and colour to the sauce. In Italy, particularly in Sicily, chocolate is often added to *agrodolce* dishes – combining sweet and sour flavours.

serves 4 as a stew, plus 4-6 as a pasta sauce

1 hare, weighing around 2kg, jointed
  (ask butcher to remove any small bones
  and ribs, and try to get the blood and liver)
flour
salt and pepper
4 tbsp olive oil
handful of pickled walnuts or capers
  (optional)
100g pancetta, cubed
12 shallots, finely chopped
4 garlic cloves, finely chopped
1 small fennel bulb, cored and chopped
3 large carrots, chopped

50g real dark chocolate or 25g
  unsweetened cocoa
2 large 400g tins of chopped tomatoes
  (if making into pasta sauce)
big handful of roughly chopped parsley

for the marinade

1 bottle of good red wine
6 bay leaves
5 whole star anise
½ tsp fennel seeds (optional)

to serve as a pasta sauce

500g tagliatelle, cooked
pesto sauce, to dress
freshly grated Parmesan cheese

You can eat this as a casserole first, then use the leftovers for a pasta sauce. Either way, start by marinating the hare overnight (time permitting) in the wine, with the bay leaves, star anise and fennel seeds, if using.

Dry off the hare, dust it with the seasoned flour and brown each piece in a little of the oil in a heavy-bottomed pan. Then add the marinade (with a little water, if necessary, to cover) and the pickled walnuts, bring to the boil and simmer for as long as it takes the hare to become really tender – this can actually be anything from 1 to 8 hours, depending on the age and condition of the hare.

While the hare is cooking, dry-fry the pancetta until golden, then add the shallots, garlic, fennel, carrots and the remaining olive oil, and sauté slowly until the carrots are tender. Add all of these to the hare together with the chocolate or cocoa and simmer for a further 15 minutes.

If serving as 'jugged hare', the blood and liver should be liquidized and added with the chocolate. Adjust the seasoning to taste. Mashed potatoes, and roast root vegetables, like beetroot and parsnips, would suit this dish.

If you are planning to serve the hare as a ragu, after cooking it in the marinade until tender, take the pieces of hare out the sauce and remove any bones, the star anise and the bay leaves. Cook until reduced somewhat. Meanwhile, in a food processor, chop the leg meat finely, then shred the saddle (not in the processor), leaving some reasonably big pieces. Return the chopped meat to the sauce and add the cooked onion mixture, the tomatoes, parsley and chocolate. Cook until the sauce has reduced and is thick and rich-looking. Adjust the seasoning to taste. Serve with tagliatelle dressed with some pesto and sprinkled with freshly grated Parmesan.

mexican refried beans with chocolate sauce

This is a variation on the Venezuelan staple *caraotas*. Eaten 'out there' (as the colonials would say), it is usually served as a breakfast dish, with *arepas*, a kind of white maize griddle cake, white cheese and fried eggs. At home, we often have this as a brunch dish. It takes a few days to make, and tastes best after three or four days. If you don't have much time, you can pressure-cook the beans without even pre-soaking them. This way you can cook them one day and eat them the next.

You can serve these with many other things, chicken, soft tortillas, scrambled, poached or fried eggs with chocolate vinegar (see the pan-seared chicken recipe on page 71), bacon, crumbly white cheese such as Wensleydale – the cheese recently been given such a boost by Wallace & Grommit.

250g small black beans from South
  America (not black-eye beans)
2 red onions, roughly chopped
3 garlic cloves, roughly chopped
1 tbsp olive oil
15g butter
good 5cm chunk of very fresh ginger,
  chopped finely or grated

1 fresh red chilli pepper, deseeded and
  finely chopped, or more to taste
200ml tomato passata
salt and pepper
25g unsweetened cocoa powder or
  chocolate
fresh coriander leaves or flat-leaf
  parsley, to garnish

Two days ahead, put the beans to soak in cold water overnight.

Next day, drain, cover with fresh water, bring to a simmer and cook gently until really tender. Gently sauté the onions and garlic in olive oil and butter for 10 minutes or so, until golden. Add the ginger and chilli, and cook for a minute or two, then add the drained cooked beans and the passata. Season with salt and pepper and leave overnight for the flavours to develop.

Next day, simmer gently for an hour. Stir in the cocoa or chocolate and garnish with the coriander just before serving.

roast lamb with chocolate, anchovy and capers

This is a very rich dish, I would recommend serving it with steamed basmati rice or new potatoes and a green salad.

serves 8-10

1 whole leg of lamb, about 2-3kg

1 large onion, roughly, chopped

small bunch of fresh rosemary

head of lavender (optional)

sprig or two of fresh thyme

30g dark chocolate or unsweetened
  cocoa

for the marinade

1 glass of red wine or sherry

1 tsp good olive oil

30g tiny capers

2 tsp strong Dijon mustard

4-6 anchovy fillets (bottled or tinned)

handful of chopped parsley or
  coriander

2 large garlic cloves

black pepper

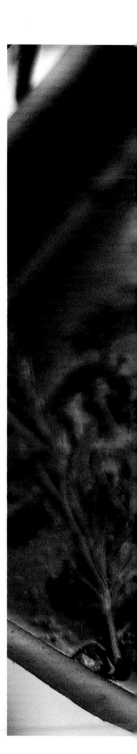

If you have time to marinate the lamb overnight it will improve the flavour and texture of the meat, but even an hour will make a difference. In a blender, make a marinade with the wine or sherry, oil, capers, mustard, anchovies, parsley, garlic and pepper. With a sharp knife, make slashes in the lamb every 5–6cm about 1cm deep. Massage the marinade into the lamb, put into a dish or baking tray, cover with foil and leave in a cool place.

When ready to cook, preheat the oven to 190°C/Gas 5. Put the chopped onion in a small mound at the bottom of the baking tray with a sprig of rosemary and the lavender if using. Put the lamb on top of the onions, which act as 'gravy browning'. Sprinkle the rest of the rosemary and thyme on top of the meat. Put in the oven and bake for 20 minutes per 500g, for pink, 30 for medium, or until cooked to taste. When ready, take it out of the oven and leave to stand in a warm place loosely covered with foil, for 10–15 minutes.

Make a gravy by scraping up the onion and any other juices and sediment in the tin. Take out the rosemary and add more wine if you like. When you have a thickish sauce, add the chocolate or cocoa and stir in well; it should thicken the sauce a little and give a deep colour and aroma. Strain or simply remove any very burnt pieces of onion before serving.

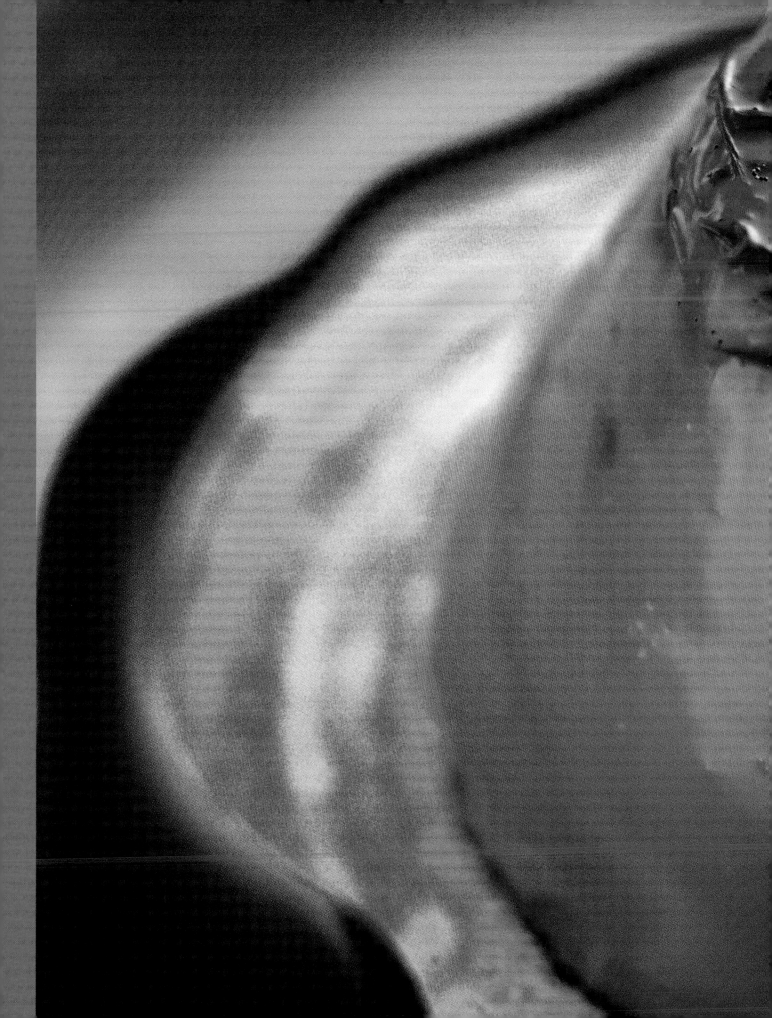

puddings, desserts & drinks

river cafe chocolate nemesis revisited

I have long admired the River Café from a distance and via the books of Rose Gray and Ruth Rogers. They have a wonderfully clear vision of how to prepare and serve food at its best, and have certainly revolutionized many kitchens in the UK and around the world. There seems hardly to be a self-respecting chef in England who has not worked there at some time in their career.

I had a surprise birthday lunch there recently, and was absolutely delighted when Ruth Rogers came to the table and declared Rococo to be her favourite shop. She then took me to meet Rose Gray and we talked chocolate for some time. Which chocolate did I use? What do they use? We all tasted some pretty raw chocolate that they had been given, and were experimenting with, from a plantation in Venezuela. Even in its raw state, the quality of the cocoa beans shone through the chocolate.

I had been dying to taste their celebrated Chocolate Nemesis, and so we shared it for pudding. At the end of the meal Ruth and Rose asked me what I thought of the pudding. Here I was, in front of these two gurus of modern Italian food, being asked my opinion of one of their most famous creations. I said it was really delicious, extremely rich and filling (we were unable to finish it), the texture sublime, but that I found it perhaps a little too sweet and buttery. Finally I asked if, with their blessing, I could tweak the recipe and put it into my book. I have changed the method of assembling the ingredients, but it seemed to produce the right texture, so here it is.

makes 6 large or 12 normal portions

100g icing sugar

250g real dark chocolate (I used Valrhona Guanaja 70%), roughly chopped

150g butter, cut into small pieces, plus more for greasing

4 organic eggs, separated

pinch of salt

1 tsp cider vinegar

crème fraîche, to serve

Preheat the oven to 180°C/Gas 4 and line the base of a 20cm round cake tin (not springform) about 5cm deep with greaseproof paper, then butter that.

Put two-thirds of the sugar in a heavy-based pan with 5 tablespoons of water. Heat until the sugar has completely dissolved then, over a low heat, add the chocolate and stir until it has melted. Finally, stir in the butter. You should have a thick, glossy mixture. Remove from the heat.

Whisk the remaining sugar with the egg white and salt and vinegar (I don't know why this works but it does seem to help), until they have reached meringue/soft peak consistency. Beat the egg yolks into the lukewarm chocolate mixture and add this mixture to your meringue bit by bit, folding it in gently.

Bring to the boil a large kettleful of water and pour into a baking tray large enough to hold the cake tin to make a bain-marie. Pour the batter into the prepared mould and place it in the baking tray filled with hot water. It is important that the water comes up to the rim of the tin. Carefully place in the hot oven and bake for 30 minutes, or until set. Test by placing you hand gently on the surface, or with a skewer; it should be set like a firm jelly.

Allow to cool out of the water bath before unmoulding. Serve cold with crème fraîche.

storing chocolate

Chocolate should always be stored in a cool dry place, away from strong smells as it absorbs flavours very easily. If you live in a very hot climate, you may have to store it in the refrigerator. Before doing so, wrap it well in plastic and put it in a hermetically sealed container. Allow it to come back to room temperature very slowly before unwrapping it. Think of a bottle of wine coming out of the fridge into a warm room, condensation appears on the glass almost immediately – if this were allowed to settle on chocolate it would cause a sugar bloom (the moisture causes sugar crystals in the chocolate to migrate to the surface and then recrystallize), which would be disastrous.

Bad girl's trifle

The antithesis of a Women's Institute trifle made from sponge, tinned peaches, jelly, solid custard and a spot of sherry, this one is for bad girls. You can do a quick version using bottled or tinned pears, ready-made custard and trifle sponges, or you could go the whole hog and make your own poached pears, home-made custard and sponge – I'll leave that up to you.

Serves at least 12

200g real dark chocolate, finely chopped

150ml boiling water

3-4 tbsp Morello cherry jam

1 packet of trifle sponges (8 pieces)

2 jars of pears in their juice (about 400g
  pears, 400ml juice)

good slug of eau-de-vie de poire
  Williams or vodka

500ml pot of ready-made custard

250ml whipping cream

250ml plain full-fat thick-set yoghurt

to decorate

chocolate curls, leaves or flakes
  (page 43)

unsweetened cocoa powder

Make a water ganache (page 32) using the chopped chocolate and the boiling water, then put on one side.

Spread a thin layer of cherry jam on the trifle sponges and arrange them at the bottom of a glass trifle dish or large salad bowl. Strain the pears and keep the juice. Mix the juice with a good slug of eau-de-vie or vodka and pour over the sponges. Put a layer of pears on the sponge. Now pour the custard over the pears. Very gently pour the cooled chocolate ganache over the layer of custard. Leave to cool for an hour or so in the fridge.

Just before serving, whip the cream until reasonably stiff, mix in the yoghurt and spread on top of the chocolate. Decorate with chocolate curls, leaves and flakes, then dust with cocoa powder through a fine sieve.

white chocolate panna cotta with saffron and cardamom

This is my idea of Italian nursery food, especially combined with white chocolate. My theory is that white chocolate is one the closest things to breast milk (see page 23), at least most small children I know seem to think so. It could be served with all sorts of things other than chocolate sauce, particularly a sharp fruit, such as rhubarb or raspberry.

serves 6

2 gelatine leaves
500ml whipping cream
1 vanilla pod, split
12 whole cardamom pods, bruised

200g white chocolate, finely chopped
½ tsp saffron strands
finely grated zest of 1 lemon
Chocolate Sauce (page 33),
  to serve

In a bowl, soak the gelatine leaves in cold water until supple.

In a small heavy pan, bring the whipping cream to the boil with the vanilla pod and seeds from the cardamom pods and simmer on a very gentle heat a few minutes to infuse. Take out the vanilla pod and the cardamom, and put these to one side.

Make a ganache by pouring a little of the hot cream on to the white chocolate crumbs (see page 30). Slice open the vanilla pod and put the seeds into the ganache.

Squeeze out excess water from the gelatine leaves and drop into the remaining hot cream. Stir until completely dissolved. Stir in the saffron and leave to steep for a minute for two. Allow to cool.

Fold into the cooled ganache, sprinkling in the lemon zest as you do. Pour the mixture into 6 small timbales, clean yoghurt pots or tea cups and chill for at least 2 hours.

To serve, unmould straight from the fridge with the help of quick dip in very hot water if necessary, and accompany with some dark chocolate sauce.

mayfield muddle

This is my version of the famous pudding 'Eton Mess'. Mayfield is the convent school where I was incarcerated for the 'best years of my life'. I hated this school with a passion. There were happy moments, of course, often involving chocolate. I made good friends there and found other kindred spirits who were happy to join in any subversive activities, like breaking into the domestic science building and making chocolate pancakes.

The foundress of the convent was an American called Cornelia Connelly (referred to irreverently by the girls as 'Corny Con'). She was married with five children, but she and her husband had both taken holy orders. In 1846, she was sent from Rome by Pope Gregory XVI to Derby in England, where she founded her first convent. The story went that one of the lowly nuns from the kitchen came on bended knee to the mother foundress, and begged for a farthing to buy some cloves for the apple pie. Corny Con is

reputed to have laughed and said, 'No – leave it to me.' She then ordered a hundred-weight of cloves – which were still being used when I was at school during the 1970s. The apple pies where certainly riddled with cloves and, as they are an expensive spice, I suspect that there must have been some truth in the tale.

This is a pretty wicked pudding but, in fact, it doesn't contain too much fat (apart from the cream and nuts), and has loads of fresh fruit.

serves 6-8

200g real dark chocolate

200ml boiling water

2-3 soft but, not too ripe, mangoes

6 passion fruit

200g double cream, whipped to stiff
peaks

200ml plain thick set yoghurt

for the meringue

150g icing sugar

whites of 4 eggs

25g unsweetened cocoa powder,
plus more for dusting

100g ground almonds

oil, for greasing

Make the meringue: first preheat the oven to 100°C/Gas ¼. Whisk a spoonful of sugar into the egg whites and start to beat. When they start to inflate, add the remaining sugar, bit by bit, until smooth, glossy and standing in soft peaks. Mix in the cocoa and almonds. Spread into a rough sheet or pipe into nests on a sheet of oiled greaseproof paper. (You can buy reuseable silicone sheets that don't need greasing for about £10.) Bake for 4 hours until dry and crisp. This will make almost double what you need, but this meringue will keep for a long time, so it can be made in advance and kept in an airtight container.

While the meringue is baking, make a water ganache with the chocolate and 200ml water as described on page 32. Allow it to cool for a couple of hours at least until thick.

Break about half the meringue into bite-sized pieces. Cube the mango flesh. Cut the passion fruit in half and squeeze into the same bowl. Mix together the cream and yoghurt.

In large glasses, layer the meringue, chocolate, fruit mixture and the yoghurt and cream. Dust with unsweetened cocoa powder and serve.

pears with vanilla ice-cream and spicy chocolate sauce

I have known Hannah as long as I can remember. My father, Tony, and Hannah's mother, Margaret, used to do 'fire watching' from the rooftop of Manchester University at the end of World War II, and the two families have remained close friends ever since. Recently, Hannah's father, Peter, 'came out' as having been a spy during the war. He is now allowed to talk about it as he has been released from his sworn secrecy after 50 years. He worked for MI6 (British Intelligence Services), sending coded messages back to the UK from Addis Ababa, Izmir and Istanbul. This is Hannah's recipe, passed down from Margaret, who got it from Elizabeth David and, as recipes do, it has evolved on the way.

serves 4-6

for version 1 (the tame one)

- 4–6 Williams pears
- zest and juice of 1 lemon
- 100g sugar
- ½ bottle of good dry white wine
- 1 vanilla pod
- 6 whole green cardamom pods

for version 2 (the spicy one)

- 4–6 Conference pears
- zest and juice of 1 lemon
- 100g sugar
- bottle of good full-bodied red wine
- 1 whole chilli pepper
- piece of cinnamon
- 5–6 cloves
- 2–3 star anise
- 1–2 cardamom pods

to serve

- Chocolate Sauce (page 33)
- good-quality vanilla ice-cream

Peel the pears but leave whole with stalks intact. Cover the pears with lemon juice. In a heavy pan, dissolve the sugar in the wine and add the lemon zest and vanilla and cardamom or chilli and spices. Add the pears and cook gently until really tender. (You may have to weight them with a heatproof plate to keep them submerged.) Test the pears with a sharp knife, as cooking time can vary from 15 minutes to an hour depending on the ripeness and variety. When you remove the pears from the liquid, boil it down to a syrupy liquid. Eat warm or cold, with the syrup, chocolate sauce (see page 33) and vanilla ice-cream.

chocolate fondue

This is a simple but effective party piece. Chunks of bread or fruit of your choice may be dipped into the fondue. Ripe Williams pears, strawberries, fresh pineapple chunks, pieces of banana, nuts or brioche all work well. If you have an official fondue set, use it; otherwise, a pan or bowl will do nicely.

serves 6-8

200g real dark chocolate

175ml whipping cream

2 tbsp milk

1 loaf of soft country bread, baguette
   and/or brioche, torn into pieces

500g mixed fruits of choice (see above)

100g mixed shelled nuts (walnuts,
   Brazils, pecans)

100g marshmallows

Make a ganache with the chocolate, cream and milk as on page 30. The ganache can be prepared in advance and reheated patiently over a double boiler, or with extreme caution over the lowest heat possible – it'd be a shame to burn it. Using fondue forks or satay sticks, simply dunk the pieces of bread, fruit, nuts or marshmallows into the mixture and devour.

chocolate bombe filled with white chocolate risotto

This rice pudding is really a sweet risotto, but using the Middle Eastern repertoire of spices. I love this combination of flavours so much, perhaps because I was born in Teheran.

serves 8

200g real dark chocolate

25g butter

seeds from 10 whole green cardamom pods

400g risotto rice

freshly grated nutmeg

½ tsp real saffron strands

about 1.25 litres milk

200g white chocolate, chopped

4 tbsp rose water (I used Lebanese or Persian)

grappa (optional)

Firstly, prepare the bombe shell(s). Temper the dark chocolate as described on pages 40-42. Pour into a 1.2 litre pudding basin or eight 150ml individual moulds and tip out the excess. This is the same process as moulding the trees (page 46). You need to do this twice to get a reasonably thick layer, allowing it just to set in between. If you are making the one large mould, then you may have some chocolate left over (I'm sure you'll find a use for it). Leave to cool for 15 minutes, then refrigerate for 30 minutes to crisp up.

Make the risotto: melt the butter in a heavy-based pan over a low heat and gently stir in the cardamom seeds and rice, being careful not to let the butter brown. Grate a good piece of nutmeg and add this and the saffron to the milk in another pan and warm gently until it is just about boiling. Add a ladleful of the hot milk to the rice and stir it in. Keep stirring so it does not stick or get lumpy, adding more ladlefuls as it is absorbed, for 20 minutes or so. The rice should be tender but still have some bite, and there should be plenty of the milky sauce. Add the white chocolate (as you would the butter and cheese to a savoury risotto), together with the rose water and a slug of grappa if you like. Stir in.

Either allow to cool and serve upside-down in the bombe case(s) or let cool a little and, when everyone is ready with bowls and spoons, pour the warm pudding into the unmoulded case(s) and invert on to a plate. The case(s) will melt fairy rapidly and surround the pudding in a veil of dark chocolate.

classic chocolate mousse

I first tried this recipe under the auspices of Thierry Dumouchel, the chocolate chef who worked with the Chocolate Society in its early days. It is his mother's recipe, made and enjoyed over many years. For me, it was a revelation as it is so simple, with consistent results every time. A soft smooth chocolate mousse based on the ganache principle.

serves 8

250g real dark chocolate, broken into pieces

50g unsalted butter, softened

whites of 9 very fresh eggs, plus 6 egg yolks

125g caster sugar

Place the broken chocolate in a heatproof bowl. Melt the chocolate in the oven on a very low heat (75–100°C/Gas ¼). It should melt in about 5 minutes – keep checking it with a fork. When melted, take out of the oven and beat with the butter in a large bowl until smooth and light.

Using an electric beater, whisk the egg whites until frothy. Add a tablespoon of sugar and continue beating on a low setting. When the egg whites are stiff, slowly shake in the remaining sugar, and continue beating slowly. If you are too quick, the eggs will liquefy. Beat the meringue to make it strong and elastic, then mix in the egg yolks.

Stir half the egg mixture into the chocolate and butter mix. Fold in the remaining egg with a large wooden spoon, working in from the outside, slowly and calmly. You need not worry about the mousse setting while you work, because the butter keeps it soft.

Pour into a large soufflé dish or 8 individual ramekins and refrigerate until set, about 2 hours or overnight.

semifreddo

In fact, this is much the same recipe as I have used for my version of the River Café Chocolate Nemesis on page 87! The method of cooking and serving it result in a very different pudding, which I think should be eaten hot.

serves 6-8

100g icing sugar

4 very fresh eggs, separated

pinch of salt

150g butter

250g real dark chocolate, chopped into small pieces

vanilla ice-cream, to serve

Put 5 tablespoons of water and half the sugar in a small pan and warm slowly until the sugar has dissolved completely.

While the sugar is dissolving, beat the egg whites with a pinch of salt and the rest of the sugar, until they have the consistency of a soft meringue.

Now add the butter and chocolate to the syrup, and stir until a smooth melted consistency is achieved. Beat in the egg yolks, and finally fold in the whites bit by bit.

Spoon the mixture into flexible ovenproof moulds (I use special ovenproof flexible plastic doughnut moulds from Lakeland) and freeze until solid, about 2 hours or overnight.

When the mixture is frozen, preheat your oven to its hottest possible setting. Put the frozen mixture into the oven and bake for 5 minutes. Check to see how it's doing - if it's well cooked on the edges, but not in the middle, it is just right!

You can serve immediately with vanilla ice-cream or refreeze and serve frozen – if you can resist the temptation.

dark chocolate and cherry 'creme brulee'

Crème brûlée is one of the all-time greats in the pudding repertoire. Sometimes, when faced with a choice of a chocolate pudding or a crème brûlée, it can be an agonizing decision. Here, there is no contest! This version, devised to incorporate chocolate, is also so much easier to make than a classic crème brûlée.

serves 8

500g very dark cherries, preferably
  Morello if available, stoned
finely grated zest of 1 lemon

500ml crème fraîche
200g real dark chocolate, finely chopped
about 250g white caster sugar

Put the stoned cherries into the bottom of 8 small ramekin dishes and sprinkle with the lemon zest.

Bring the cream to the boil and make a ganache with the cream and chocolate as described on page 30. Pour the ganache mixture over the cherries and chill for at least 2 hours.

Heat the sugar and 6 tablespoons of water in a pan until you have a bubbling caramel mixture. Let settle briefly, then spoon carefully over the chilled pots of cherry and ganache, it should set instantly as soon as it comes into contact with the cold mixture.

These are best served immediately.

light chocolate mousse

serves 4-6

400ml whipping cream
250g real dark chocolate, finely chopped

Prepare a ganache with the 250ml of the whipping cream and the chocolate as described on page 30. Allow the mixture to cool to about 35°C (approximately blood temperature, if you don't have a thermometer).

Whip the remaining cream until standing in soft peaks and about doubled in volume, then mix very quickly into the ganache with a balloon whisk. The result should be a rather liquid ganache; if not, the ganache was too cold (return it briefly to the bain-marie). Pour into 4–6 ramekins and chill for several hours before serving.

marquise au chocolat

The marquise is a classic chocolate pudding. This version uses the light chocolate mousse as its centre, but there is much scope for experimentation. You might try a version using 650g of water, tea or coffee ganache (see page 32), so no cream is used.

serves 10-12

slug of very good rum (rhum agricole
from Martinique), or other strong booze
1 mug of strong cold espresso coffee

1-2 packets of boudoir biscuits (at least
30 fingers)
1 recipe quantity Light Chocolate Mousse
(see above)
custard or melted ice-cream, to serve

Butter a 1.5 litre loaf tin and line it with greaseproof paper. Mix the alcohol into the coffee. Dip the boudoir biscuits into the boozy coffee until they are well soaked and use to line the prepared tin, leaving the ends open. Pour in the mousse, cover with a layer of the dipped biscuits and leave to chill overnight.

Invert to unmould (first giving it a quick dip in warm water if necessary) and cut into slices. Float the slices on a layer of cold freshly made custard or melted real vanilla ice-cream to serve.

dairy- and wheat-free chocolate roulade

For some reason, I seem to be surrounded by people with special dietary requirements, so I dreamed up this basic pudding. If you don't have any problems with dairy produce and want to add a layer of whipped cream, go ahead. Allow yourself free rein to experiment with the ganache; you can make it with water, tea or coffee (see page 32), and add cardamom, orange flower water, a drop of essential oil or some bits of fruit or some booze. Using a water, tea or coffee ganache also makes it very low in fat.

serves 8

for the ganache

200g real dark chocolate

200ml liquid of your choice (see above)

for the génoise sponge

25g unsweetened cocoa powder, plus more to dust

100g icing sugar

4 eggs, separated

100g ground almonds, plus more to dust

Make the ganache as described on page 32. Let cool and then chill for about 2 hours.

To make the sponge: preheat the oven to 180°C/Gas 4. Sift the cocoa and sugar together and beat with the egg whites to a soft peak meringue. Fold in the almonds, followed by the egg yolks. Try to keep as much air in the mix as you can. Spread on a silicone baking sheet on a large baking tray and bake for 10–15 minutes. Let cool.

Turn out on a piece of greaseproof paper dusted with ground almonds. Spread the ganache over it and roll up like a Swiss roll. Dust with cocoa powder and more ground almonds.

paul de bondt's chocolate roulade

serves 8

for the chocolate génoise

75g 00 (Italian doppio zero) flour

25g unsweetened cocoa powder, plus
   more to serve

4 eggs, separated

pinch of salt

100g sugar

for the filling

soft berries and crème fraîche, etc.

Coffee, Tea, or Water Ganache
(pages 30-32)

to serve

icing sugar

Preheat the oven to 200°C/Gas 6. Line a rectangular baking tray (about 30x 40cm) with greaseproof paper. Sieve the flour and cocoa powder together. Beat the egg whites with the salt and sugar, until they attain a meringue consistency. Mix in the egg yolks, then fold in the flour and cocoa slowly to keep as much air in the mix as possible. Spoon into the prepared tray and bake for 12 minutes or until just cooked through (the tip of a knife inserted into it will come out dry). It must not be overcooked or it will become too dry.

When the cake is cool, turn out of the tray and remove the lining paper. Spread the ganache over it, followed by the chosen filling. Roll it up like a Swiss roll and dust with cocoa powder and icing sugar.

orange and geranium pots

A couple of years ago I went to Seville in January for the first time. It was very cold and crisp, with glorious blue skies. I suppose I should have expected to see oranges, but I was bowled over by the number of orange trees in fruit planted on all the streets. I was being even more dense when I pondered why no one scrumped these ripe oranges. The penny dropped when we picked one and tasted it - it was too bitter to eat, but just the job for marmalade. On the last morning of our stay, the Christmas lights were being taken down, and there were hundreds of windfalls lying all over the street. I could not resist the opportunity to tidy a couple of kilos into a bag and take them back to London to make marmalade. Choose your favourite oranges - it could be very tart blood oranges, or even one Seville orange mixed with some sweet oranges.

This recipe can be also be made with cream (see Chocolate Tea Pots, page 113) or, if you want to take a risk and make a really extreme pudding, try this one - it's a bit of a dare!

serves 6

200g real dark chocolate

200g freshly squeezed orange juice (oranges vary in juiciness, so it is difficult to specify a number)

about 100g icing sugar to taste, if necessary (depending on the sweetness of the oranges)

drop of pure geranium essential oil

1 tsp orange flower water

Finely chop the chocolate and put it into a heatproof bowl. Scald the orange juice by heating it in a small pan until boiling. Add sugar if necessary at this stage. Add the geranium oil to the hot juice. Be careful when measuring the oil, some bottles allow just one drop to be dispensed, others are not so predictable. It's probably worth dropping the oil on to a spoon, just in case…

Make a ganache by pouring the boiling juice, bit by bit, on to the chopped chocolate (see page 30). When you have blended in all the juice, add the orange flower water to the ganache. Pour into small coffee cups, glasses or ramekins and chill for at least 2 hours.

chocolate tea pots

This is one of the simplest and most delicious chocolate pudding recipes I have ever made. The scalded cream cooks the chocolate, and the tea adds a delicate perfume. The texture is sublime, and it is one of the simplest forms of ganache.

serves 8

125g real dark chocolate

400ml single cream

1 tbsp best-quality Earl Grey tea

1 tsp orange flower water

Finely chop the chocolate and put it into a large heatproof bowl. Scald the cream by bringing it to the boil. Add the tea and leave to stand for 2 minutes; strain.

Pour the cream bit by bit on to the chocolate. Use a rubber spatula to stir it in, ensuring a smooth emulsion. (If it gets too cool to melt the chocolate, you may have to heat it gently again.) Add the orange flower water.

Pour into small coffee cups, glasses or ramekins and chill for at least 2 hours.

chocolat a l'ancienne (old-fashioned hot chocolate)

The secret recipe of Rosa Cannabich, a contemporary of Mozart, this is a wonderfully silky drink that I first tasted at a performance of 'Mozart au Chocolat'. It was served to the 'Court' audience in the inner sanctum during a performance at the ICA in London. The staging was such that a set was built with windows, and some of the seats for the audience were in that inner chamber, while the poor miserable rabble outside could only look through the windows and did not get to taste the chocolate. Mozart is reputed to have drunk this hot chocolate at Mannheim in 1778. Although this recipe seems to break all the cardinal rules about heating chocolate and adding liquid, it does work and is almost a meal in itself!

serves 4

180g real dark chocolate

50ml crème fraîche

pinch of salt

500 l milk

2 tbsp dark rum

50ml cold espresso coffee

To make the grated chocolate decoration, put the chocolate in the freezer for 2 hours to harden. Grate off 20g with a sharp knife or a potato peeler.

Beat the crème fraîche with an electric hand-held beater, until stiff, but not butter! Chill until you are ready to serve the chocolate.

Finely chop the remaining chocolate and place in a saucepan with the salt and 50ml water. Melt over a low heat, stirring constantly and taking great care that it does not burn or the flavour will be ruined. When the chocolate is smooth and shiny, stir in the milk and then the sugar, if using. Bring to the boil, then simmer for 5 minutes. Be very careful because the chocolate bubbles up and thickens rapidly. Stir in the rum and coffee and boil 2 minutes longer. Beat the chocolate with a whisk to lighten it.

When ready to serve, add a spoonful of the whipped crème fraîche and top with the grated chocolate. In the summer, this is delicious served chilled.

chocolate vodka or gin and chocolate martinis

Noilly Prat dry white vermouth

lots of ice cubes

cocktail olives or onions and/or strips of

lemon peel (optional) or crushed ice

for the chocolate vodka or gin

1 bottle (700ml) of vodka or gin

140g real dark chocolate, grated or

pulverized

Make the chocolate gin or vodka, according to your preference, by melting the chocolate (see page 32) and pouring into the bottle (you may have to drink a little to make some room), resealing and shaking vigorously.

To make the chocolate martinis: in a cocktail shaker mix 2 parts vermouth to 1 of chocolate vodka or gin, with lots of ice.

Shake or stir, according to preference, and serve in chilled martini glasses, with cocktail olives or onions and/or strips of lemon peel or just crushed ice, if you feel like it.

chocolate manhattans

Make chocolate bourbon, as in the Chocolate Martini recipe above, using bourbon instead of gin or vodka.

Shake one part with two parts of red martini and some crushed ice, add a cocktail cherry and serve in a straight-sided whisky tumbler.

biscuits, cakes & breads

classic chocolate chip biscotti

I saw these being made at a charity wine auction in a *palazzo* near Frantoia, outside Florence.
I suppose it was an Italian equivalent to a church fête, but conducted with great aplomb.

makes about 30

250g soft lightly salted butter
250g brown sugar
125g white sugar

3 eggs
550g 00 (Italian doppio zero) flour, sifted
2 tsp real vanilla essence
200-350g real dark chocolate chips or
    roughly cut pieces of real dark chocolate

Preheat the oven to 180°C/Gas 4 and line a baking tray with a silicone baking sheet or
greaseproof paper. In a large bowl, cream the butter and sugars, then beat in the eggs.
Add the flour, spoonful by spoonful. When all mixed in, add the vanilla and chocolate
chips or pieces. Spoon the mixture on the prepared baking tray in 2 parallel oblongs,
spaced well apart to allow for spreading. You may need more than one baking tray.

Bake for 35–40 minutes until just brown on the edges. Remove from oven and let cool a
little (leaving oven on). Cut the oblongs across into 1.5cm thick biscotti and return to the
oven. Switch off and leave the biscotti in until they're cold, turning after 20 minutes.

stolen sardinian chocolate tart

This recipe was stolen from a famous restaurant in Sardinia, which shall remain unnamed,
as will the perpetrator! Made without flour or almonds, it is so good it had to be shared.

serves 10

200g real dark chocolate
120g unsalted butter, plus more for the tin

8 eggs, separated
170g caster sugar
30g unsweetened cocoa powder
1 tiny cup of very strong espresso coffee

Melt the chocolate in a bowl in a very low oven for about 5–10 minutes (melting chocolate, page 32). Turn the oven up to 180°C/Gas 4 and butter a 25cm round springform tin. Whisk the egg whites with the sugar to soft peak/meringue consistency.

Stir the butter into the melted chocolate, then add the egg yolks, cocoa powder and coffee. When it is all smooth and well mixed to a ganache consistency (page 30), fold in the egg whites, bit by bit, until all are amalgamated.

Pour the mixture into the prepared tin and bake for 30 minutes, or until a knife inserted into the centre of the cake comes out clean. Allow to cool in the tin.

chocolate brownies

This is Mandy's recipe for brownies, which are fabulously fudgy. Mandy read Italian at Bristol University, where she met my husband James. She then married an Italian air steward and now lives in 'la Dolce Vita' territory near Ostia Lido, outside Rome. She leads a whirlwind life, now as Supermum, single-handedly bringing up three children, guiding groups of Americans around Rome, and making these famous brownies!

makes about 24 pieces

350g butter

140g unsweetened cocoa powder

6 eggs

675g caster sugar

250g plain flour

3 tsp real vanilla essence

100g shelled fresh walnuts, roughly
   chopped

Preheat the oven to 180°C/Gas 4 and line a fairly deep baking tray about 20 x 30cm with greaseproof paper. In a large heavy pan, melt the butter with the cocoa. Whisk the eggs, then whisk in the sugar, followed by the flour and vanilla. Finally, add the cocoa and butter mixture, and the nuts. Pour into the prepared tray and bake for 40–45 minutes until springy to the touch. Do not overcook, or you'll loose the fudginess. Cut into squares while warm and leave to cool.

vegan chocolate biscotti

It can be daunting cooking for vegans, often one thinks of tofu and seaweed and how joyless this kind of repertoire can be in the wrong hands. Vegan seems to imply sacrifice and self-denial. There are, of course, many luxurious ingredients that can be included in the vegan repertoire and often chocolate is overlooked, which is a shame. There should never be any dairy products or animal fats in pure dark chocolate (as I discuss on page 17, some manufacturers actually put animal fats into dark chocolate – unforgivable!) and, as chocolate is so rich in vitamins and minerals, it ought to be an essential food supplement.

This is an incredibly quick and simple Tuscan recipe that I watched being cooked at the same event as the classic chocolate chip cookies. In Italy, biscotti simply means 'biscuit', but the Siennese ones with which we are now so familiar are, of course, usually served with a glass of *vin santo* for dipping.

makes about 35

250g 00 (Italian doppio zero) flour

100g caster sugar

100g real dark chocolate, chopped into pieces

40g fresh pine nuts or walnuts

small pinch of salt

½ sachet of dried yeast (3.5g)

75ml mild but good-quality extra-virgin olive oil

100ml vin santo (available from Italian delis or a good wine merchant)

Preheat the oven to 180°C/Gas 4 and line 2–3 baking sheets with greaseproof paper.

Put the flour, sugar, chocolate, nuts, salt and yeast in a bowl. Mix well, then add the oil and vin santo, and mix them in.

Spoon walnut-sized pieces on to the prepared baking trays, leaving plenty of space between them for spreading, and bake for 8-10 minutes until just firm.

chocolate and gingerbread men and beasts

The whole process of making these can keep the children happy for at least an hour!

makes about 12

100g golden syrup

1 egg

350g 00 (Italian doppio zero) flour

1 tsp ground cinnamon

1 tsp ground ginger

½ tsp ready-ground cardamom

1 tsp bicarbonate of soda

1 tsp unsweetened cocoa powder

100g butter

100g chopped real chocolate pieces

140g golden brown caster sugar

Smarties and white icing, to decorate
 (optional)

Preheat the oven to 200°C/Gas 6 and line several baking trays with greaseproof paper or silicone baking sheets.

Beat the egg into the golden syrup in a bowl. Sift the flour, then mix in the spices, bicarbonate of soda and cocoa powder. Put this into a food processor (you can also do this in a bowl if you prefer) and add the butter. Mix together until the mixture resembles fine crumbs. Add the chocolate, sugar, syrup and egg mixture, and mix until a smooth dough is formed. If the mixture looks too dry, add a teaspoon or two of cold water.

Roll out, using extra flour if needed (you shouldn't need it), to a thickness of about 3mm and cut out shapes, either with a cutter or freehand. Put on the prepared baking trays and bake for 10–15 minutes until cooked and starting to brown at the edges and smell cooked (take care not to overcook). Allow to cool on a wire rack and decorate with Smarties and white icing if you wish.

epiphany chocolate tart

The feast of the epiphany seems to be celebrated in most Latin countries, and hardly at all anywhere else. I love the idea of the ceremony to celebrate the arrival of the three kings. Although they did not bring almonds, they do seem to be in all the epiphany cakes I've ever eaten – the white chocolate was my idea.

served 8-10

1 recipe quantity Chocolate Pastry (see page 130-32)

200g white chocolate

100g almonds

50g soft white bread, ground into breadcrumbs (I've used pitta bread – it was all I had, but it worked admirably)

1 lemon, preferably unwaxed organic

2 eggs, separated

pinch of salt

3 tbsp apricot jam

good handful of black cherries (with or without the stones; leave them in for more flavour, but do then warn people!)

Butter a fairly deep, round loose-bottomed pie tin (4 x 23cm). Roll out the pastry and use it to line the tin, or simply mould it in with the fingers. Leave to rest in the fridge. Melt the chocolate in an ovenproof bowl in a very low oven (50°C) for 5 minutes. Don't overheat!

Turn the oven up to 150°C/Gas 2 and bake the almonds until lightly toasted. Chop in a food processor until ground quite small, but they don't need to be smooth. Turn the oven up to 180°C/Gas 4. Set half the almonds aside. Add the bread to the remaining half and process until well mixed. Zest the lemon and juice it (take out pips). Beat the egg whites with a pinch of salt until they form soft peaks. Into the melted white chocolate, beat the egg yolks, followed by the lemon juice and zest, and the almonds and breadcrumb mixture. Fold in the egg whites.

Take the pastry case out of the fridge and spread the bottom with apricot jam. Dot the cherries over that, then sprinkle over the remaining ground almonds. Cover with the batter and bake in the oven for 45 minutes, or until a knife inserted into the middle comes out clean and dry. Serve warm or cold.

torta-mousse al cioccolato

This is my Italian teacher's favourite cake recipe. Annelise is a great cook and a brilliant Italian teacher – we insist that we cook together regularly as part of the course. The lesson after she had given me this recipe, I thought I'd better make it and take it along for a critique, and when I arrived I found that she too had made the cake, so we were able to use it as an exercise in comparatives. I'm afraid I had the advantage, as my cake was still warm and hers had been made the day before.

My ability as a linguist is somewhat limited, but I try hard not to become one of the 'let them speak English' brigade. I have grown to love Italy more with each visit. The Italians understand so well how to create the perfect welcome, which normally involves delicious simple fresh food in season, which I find a great inspiration. There is now a growing movement, Slow Food, set up as a protest when McDonalds opened in the Piazza di Spagna in Rome. It has saved many small artisan producers from going out of business, and preaches the gospel that food should be enjoyed in context and at the right pace.

serves 8-10

150g butter, cubed, plus more for greasing

50g plain flour, sifted, plus more for dusting

300g real dark chocolate

5 eggs, separated

100g icing sugar

Preheat the oven to 200°C/Gas 6 and butter and flour a 24cm springform cake tin. Melt the chocolate as described on page 32. Mix the butter into the melted chocolate. In a large bowl, beat the egg yolks with half the sugar, then add the melted chocolate and the flour.

Finally, beat the egg whites with the remaining sugar until stiff (or meringue) and fold them into the mixture. Pour into the prepared cake tin and bake in the oven for about 15–20 minutes, until it feels firm when touched with palm of the hand. It's very important not to overcook this cake, because it should be very moist. When you take it out of the oven it will have risen a bit like a soufflé, but then it will deflate.

raspberry and chocolate tart

I was taken for a surprise birthday lunch to the Waterside Inn, when my son was a babe in arms. He should not have been there at all, but had been crying all morning and would not be left with anyone – we had no choice but to take him or cancel lunch. I was very nervous about the reception we would get in this very smart Michelin-starred restaurant (three at that time) when rolling up with an infant. In fact, he was in marvellous humour when we arrived, and we were all welcomed like long-lost friends. The Europeans definitely understand that children, however young, should be encouraged in gastronomy. I chose the chocolate and raspberry tart for pudding, and it was sublime. This is my attempt to recreate it.

serves 8-10

vanilla ice-cream, to serve

1 recipe quantity Chocolate Pastry (pages 130–32)
450g raspberries
vanilla icing sugar, to dust
cream, crème anglaise or the best real

for the ganache
300g real dark chocolate, plus more for the base
300ml whipping cream or crème fraîche

Make the pastry, use it to line a tart tin and bake blind as described on pages 130-32 for about 20 minutes, or until cooked. Leave to cool.

Make the ganache as described on page 30. When the pastry is cool and the ganache has cooled to a thick custard-like consistency, arrange most of the raspberries on the pastry base, keeping a good handful back for serving.

You could paint the cooked pastry base with a thin layer of melted/tempered (pages 40–42) chocolate if you can be bothered, but you don't need to. Pour the ganache over the raspberries and leave in the fridge to set for at least a couple of hours.

Serve with the remaining raspberries piled on the top and dusted with vanilla icing sugar. Serve with cream, crème anglaise or the best real vanilla ice-cream.

pear and chocolate tart

This is an old favourite in our house. It has been through many incarnations and can be adapted to suit your mood. Sometimes I cook it for much longer than indicated below (it's better firmer if it's to be served warm), and sometimes I put a layer of Seville orange marmalade on the pastry base before adding the pears. This version uses a variation on the ganache theme, substituting custard for cream in the ganache. The whites of the eggs are whipped and added at the end to give an even airier effect. The whole thing is much lighter than the cream-based ganache version. If you're not worried about lightly cooked eggs, you can even use this mixture uncooked. The pastry can be made the day before, or a larger quantity can be prepared well in advance and frozen.

serves 8-10

for the chocolate pastry

- 15g unsweetened cocoa powder
- 130g very fine flour, ideally 00 (Italian doppio zero), plus more for dusting the tin
- pinch of salt
- 40g icing sugar, plus more for dusting the tart
- 85g unsalted butter, roughly cubed, plus more for greasing the tin
- 1 egg yolk

for the filling

- 2 eggs, separated
- 30g sugar
- 300ml milk
- 1 vanilla pod
- 300g real dark chocolate, finely chopped in food processor until the consistency of breadcrumbs and just beginning to melt
- 3 large or 4 small ripe but firm pears, preferably Williams

to decorate and serve

- cape gooseberries
- whipping cream, crème fraîche or vanilla ice-cream

To make the pastry, first sift the cocoa powder, flour, salt and icing sugar together. Place in a food processor with the butter, and using the metal blade, mix until fine crumbs form. Add the egg yolk and pulse gently until you have a lump of pastry. Wrap in cling film and chill for an hour or so.

When the pastry is firm, preheat the oven to 180°C/Gas 4 and generously butter and flour the base and sides of a fairly deep, round loose-bottomed pie tin (4 x 25cm). Roll the pastry out on the base and then place the base in the tin. Don't worry if the pastry breaks; it is very short and can easily be repaired. Roll out the trimmings of the pastry and use to line the sides, pressing the pastry into the corners. The top edge of the pastry can be very thin and left with quite a rough finish; it will have an attractive lacy look when baked. Prick all over with a fork and bake for 15 minutes. Put to one side to cool.

To make the filling, first prepare a custard: beat the egg yolks and sugar in a heatproof bowl. In a separate pan, bring the milk with the vanilla pod to the boil, then whisk the boiling milk into the egg mixture with a balloon whisk. Keep whisking until the mixture thickens. If the mixture is not hot enough to thicken, return it briefly to a low heat, but be very careful or you'll end up with scrambled egg! When you have a light custard (it doesn't need to be too thick), pour it little by little on to the chocolate to make the ganache, as described on page 30.

Peel the pears, cut them in half and scoop out the core and stem. Arrange the pear halves on the cooked pastry base.

Whisk the egg whites in a clean bowl (you will have 2 or 3 depending on when you made the pastry – either is fine) until forming soft peaks. Beat one-quarter into the custard, then fold the remainder in gently. Pour the mixture over the pears.

Bake for about 30 minutes, or until risen and set to your taste. You can decide whether you want a soft filling or a firmer one, depending on how long you bake it (soft is better when cold and a firmer set better for serving hot).

Decorate with cape gooseberries and dust with icing sugar. Serve hot or cold, with whipping cream, crème fraîche, or vanilla ice-cream.

chocolate pound cake with white chocolate frosting

This is based on the classic pound cake recipe. It is a very simple cake, not too rich and suitable for making on a large scale.

serves 10

100g butter, plus more for greasing

225g real dark chocolate

225g flour

3 level tsp baking powder

225g soft brown sugar

3 large eggs

225g sour cream or crème fraîche

1 tsp real vanilla essence

unsweetened cocoa powder, to dust

for the white chocolate frosting

200g real white chocolate

200ml whipping cream, crème fraîche or sour cream

Preheat the oven to 180°C/Gas 4 and butter a large kugelhopf mould (any mould will do, but keep checking as cooking times will vary in other moulds). Melt half the chocolate as described on page 32.

Sift together the flour and baking powder. Using the metal blade in the food processor, beat the butter, sugar, eggs, crème fraîche, sifted flour mixture and vanilla. When it is all mixed, add the melted chocolate and give it a final mix.

Pour the mixture into the tin and bake for 30–45 minutes, until a skewer inserted into the cake comes out clean. Allow to cool in the tin and then turn out.

To make the white chocolate frosting: first melt the white chocolate very carefully as described on page 32 (do not overheat). Beat the cream until it starts to thicken. Fold the cream into the melted chocolate as per the Ganache recipe (page 30) and chill until stiff.

Spread the frosting on the cake and dust with unsweetened cocoa powder.

sephardic chocolate and almond cake

This is a variation on Claudia Roden's recipe that has been one of our family favourites for years – another must-have at the annual family cricket match. My brother-in-law, Simon Roden, first introduced me to this cake.

serves 8-10

225g real dark chocolate
25g unsalted butter, cut into pieces, plus
   more for greasing
5 eggs, separated
170g caster sugar

125g ground almonds
2 tbsp milk
1 tsp cider vinegar

to decorate (optional)
icing sugar
cocoa powder

Melt the chocolate as described on page 32. After taking the chocolate out of the oven, turn the temperature up to 180°C/Gas 4 and butter a 25cm springform tin. Mix the butter into the melted chocolate. Whisk the egg whites with the sugar to meringue/soft peak consistency, beat in the egg yolks and then fold in the ground almonds. Fold the egg white mixture into the chocolate and butter, and finally add the milk and vinegar (the vinegar stops the cake from cracking too much when it rises).

Pour into the prepared tin and bake for 35–45 minutes, or until a skewer inserted into the cake comes out clean. Leave the cake to cool in the tin.

Turn out and sprinkle with icing sugar/cocoa powder – you can make a cardboard stencil of a hare, a lamb, or any other motif you like. First lightly dust the whole cake with cocoa powder, then lay the stencil on the cake and sieve the icing sugar through it (you can use a tea strainer, if you want to be more accurate). Lift the card away very carefully when you have finished.

Brioche with chocolate nibs

Brioche is sometimes served toasted as an accompaniment to foie gras. Here it contains cocoa nibs, which add crunch to contrast with the other textures. Chocolate Balsamic Vinegar (page 60) could also be used if the foie gras was served with some salad leaves.

makes 1 large loaf

1 tsp dried yeast

50g sugar

2 tbsp warm milk

400g 00 (Italian doppio zero) flour

pinch of salt

3 eggs, lightly beaten

150g softened butter, plus more for
 greasing

50g cocoa nibs (page 59)

The day before: In a small bowl, dissolve the yeast and 1 tablespoon of the sugar in the milk, and set aside until it starts to bubble and froth.

Sift the flour into a large bowl, then stir in the salt. Add the yeast mixture, eggs, remaining sugar and butter, and beat everything until well mixed. Leave the dough in a warm place for about 2–4 hours, or until doubled in size.

Push down the dough with a wooden spoon, then put it in a greased clean bowl, cover with cling film and leave overnight in a cool place.

In the morning, butter a large brioche or kugelhopf mould. Break down the dough and knead it briefly until all the air has been squeezed out. Knead in the cocoa nibs, then put the dough into the buttered mould and cover with cling film. Leave in a warm place for about 3–4 hours, or until the dough rises to the top of the mould (i.e. doubles in size).

Meanwhile preheat the oven to 190°C/Gas 5, then bake the brioche for 20–25 minutes, or until it is golden brown and sounds hollow when tapped on the base. (You will need to turn it out of the tin to do this.) If it is not ready, you can return it to the tin and the oven to continue cooking. Turn out and leave to cool on a wire rack.

chocolate breakfast muffins or tea loaf

This versatile recipe, an old family favourite from my mother-in-law, can be baked shaped either as muffins or as a loaf. No cricket tea is complete without the latter. This version has less sugar than the traditional one and little or no fat. The chocolate is my addition. You do need to think ahead, as it needs a sleep over! Other than that it is very quick to make and extremely simple. Serve the loaf cold, thinly sliced and buttered, with afternoon tea or for breakfast. Alternatively, use paper muffin cases and bake for about 20 minutes for a late breakfast – eat warm!

makes 8–10 muffins

100g dried fruit

50g brown sugar

200ml cold tea

butter, for greasing

1 egg

1 tbsp rich dark Seville orange
  marmalade

225g self-raising flour

1 tsp mixed spice

50g real chocolate, chopped into small
  chunks

The day before: put the fruit, sugar and tea in bowl or jug and leave overnight.

The next day, preheat the oven to 180°C/Gas 4 and grease a 500g loaf tin well or arrange 8–10 muffin cases on a baking sheet. In a large mixing bowl, beat the egg with the marmalade and add the overnight mixture of tea, sugar and fruit. Sift the flour and spice, add the chocolate and mix into the other ingredients.

Pour into the prepared tin or muffin cases and bake in the oven for 1 hour for the loaf or 20–30 minutes for the muffins, or until cooked (they spring back when pressed). Let cool in the tin or cases for 20 minutes before turning on to a wire rack to cool completely.

acknowledgements

A special thank you to Paul de Bondt. A very big thank you to: Alessandro Balestri, Roberto Bava, Michael Coe, Alan Davidson, Rose Gray, Eugenio Guarducci, Cecilia Iacobelli, Madhur Jaffrey, Tina Lambi, Monica Meschini, Claudia Roden, Ruth Rogers, Andrea Slitti and Lydia Sodani. Francoise Dietrich, Lewis Esson, Richard Foster, Jane Suthering, Thom, Emma, Katie and all the team. Jane O'Shea, Alison Cathie and all at Quadrille for their unwavering support. To my team at Rococo, especially Jo and Ruth, and to all the loyal Rococo supporters. Finally to the Coady Family, including the Booths, Galtons, and Rodens, and Kati Iglai.

bibliography

Sophie and Michael Coe **The True History of Chocolate** Thames and Hudson 1996

Frederic Bau **Au Coeur des Saveurs** Montagud Editores, Barcelona 1998

Eric Schlosser **Fast Food Nation** Allen Lane The Penguin Press 2001 [UK]

John Ashton & Suzy Ashton **A Chocolate a Day** (Keeps the Doctor away) Souvenir Press 2001

Madhur Jaffrey **Eastern Vegetarian Cooking** Jonathan Cape 1983; (paper) Arrow 1990 [UK]

Claudia Roden **Mediterranean Cookery** BBC Books 1987

list of suppliers

Rococo,
321 Kings Road,
Chelsea, London SW3 5EP
tel 020 7352 5857
www.rococochocolates.com or www.rococo.ro
Full international mail order service
(Those trying to obtain **cocoa nibs**, currently only supplied in this country by Rococo, should telephone.)

The Chocolate Society
36 Elizabeth Street,
London SW1W 9NZ
tel 020 7259 9222
mail order service (UK only) 01423 322230
www.thechocolatesociety.co.uk

The author also recommends readers look for Valrhona (www.valrhona.com), Barry Callebaut, Scharffen-berger and Green & Blacks (www.greenandblacks.com).
The best sources for real chocolate would be good delicatessens, supermarkets (especially Sainsbury, Tesco and Waitrose) or department stores, such as Fortnum & Mason, Harrods, Harvey Nichols and Selfridges.

www.chocolocate.com provide a list of worldwide chocolate and equipment suppliers.

Rococo chocolates can also be found at
The Fine Cheese Co, 29-31 Walcot Street, Bath BA1 5BN tel 01225 483407
Algerian Coffee Stores, 52 Old Compton Street, London W1V 6PB tel 020 7437 2480
East Dulwich Deli 15-17 Lordship Lane, London SE22 8EW tel 020 8693 2525
The Conran Shop Chelsea, Michelin House, Fulham Road, London SW3 6RD tel 020 7589 7401
The Conran Shop, 55 Marylebone High Street, London W1U 5HS tel 020 7723 2223
The Conran Shop Paris Rive Gauche, 117 Rue du Bac, 75007 Paris tel 1 42 84 10 01

Good suppliers of chocolate moulds, operating a mail order service, are Vantage House and Chocolate World, both at www.vantage-house.com